·FLIES FOR·
ALASKA

•FLIES FOR•
ALASKA
A GUIDE TO BUYING & TYING

•ANTHONY J. ROUTE•

Johnson Books: Boulder

Spring Creek Press: Estes Park

Dedication

To my wife
Ann Ivancich Route

Cover design: Bob Schram
Cover photographs: Robert Pollock
Photographs not otherwise credited are by the author.

ISBN 1-55566-087-8
LCCCN 91-77326

3 4 5 6 7 8 9

Printed in the United States of America by
Johnson Printing
A Division of Johnson Publishing Company
1880 South 57th Court
Boulder, Colorado 80301

Contents

Preface

Please don't use *Flies for Alaska* as you would a dictionary of fly patterns. You won't get the most from this book by simply flipping to a section on flies, nymphs for instance, that you feel like tying at the moment. For one thing, you'll find that I didn't consistently use discrete sections like those found in a standard book of patterns. It would be best to read completely through the book once and then develop your own game plan regarding what patterns you would like to tie. This way you'll grasp the overall scheme of things and be able to customize your assortment to suit your own needs.

For instance, regardless of the season in which your fishing will take place, you will most likely want some representative—whether it be an alevin or a maggot—from Chapter 1, Eggs to Flesh. Likewise you'll probably want to make standard selections from the other chapters. It is at this point that you'll be able to make the best use of the seasonal and species-related charts at the end of each chapter to create a list of patterns that you would like to tie or, in some cases, buy.

The photographs and fly recipes should be studied closely because not much in the world of fly tying is standardized, and some fly patterns may be called by other names on a regional basis. A case in point is the Lake Leech. Almost everywhere outside of Alaska, it's called the Marabou Leech. I suspect that it had its origins outside of Alaska so the name Marabou Leech probably should take precedence, but it is not my aim in this book to consider such things. I'll let it stand simply as what it is—the same fly pattern with two different names.

You should also realize that many proven patterns undergo a complete name change when even a small bit of new material is added to them. For example, add some Krystal Flash to the tail of an ordinary Wooly Bugger, and it's often called a Flash-A-Bugger. If you're familiar with the Wooly Bugger, you can probably see through the smoke and recognize a Flash-A-Bugger for what it is. I don't subscribe to the idea of changing the name of a fly if only a minor addition has been made, but I have mentioned variations of the dressing in the text.

I do, however, add a descriptive term when a major component in the original dressing has been replaced with a material different enough to warrant mentioning—a practice put forth by Eric Leiser in *The Book Of Fly Patterns*. For instance, I tie my Black Ghosts with a marabou wing instead of a hackle wing and therefore refer to the fly as a Marabou Black Ghost. By understanding these two precepts, in conjunction with a look at the photographs, you may recognize a very similar or identical pattern that is available locally for your inspection or purchase.

Incidentally, the flies photographed here are true representations of the ones that I use. I haven't spruced them up with extraordinary materials nor have I tied them on classier hooks than I regularly use. Like many other fly tiers, I will spend hours working on Atlantic salmon flies or Alaska patterns destined to be enclosed in glass on someone's office wall, but the flies discussed here are meant to be tied on the end of a leader. I don't want anyone, especially a novice fly tier, to get the impression that all the legs on a Marabou Girdle Bug have to be perfectly straight and exactly the same length. If that's something you want to strive for, so much the better, but if your time at the tying bench and on the water in Alaska is limited—and whose isn't—it would be better to have a dozen less-than-perfect Marabou Girdle Bugs than one perfect specimen.

There is one other item I need to point out. Because it is often difficult to distinguish between Arctic char and Dolly Varden without performing an autopsy, I will use the term char for both, except in the case of sea-run fish which will be called Dolly Varden. I realize lake trout are also char, but in flyfishing terms they are different enough to be dealt with separately and will be referred to as lake trout.

Acknowledgments

As I began to put together this book, I asked for a lot of help and I got it. I asked for information on origins of flies, sample flies, and samples of various tying materials. I received a lot more information and samples than I needed or could use, so even if their contributions are not present within these pages, I thank the following people and companies: Robert Borden of Hareline Dubbin; Phil Camera of Larva Lace Products; Hedron, Inc.; Andrew Kreinik of Kreinik Fly Tying Supplies; Mike Mercer of The Fly Shop; O. Mustad & Son; PAC Manufacturing and Distributing; Mark Roth; Ray Treanor of Umpqua Feather Merchants; Stephen Vletas of Westbank Anglers; Robert Weet of Angler Sport Group; Wright & McGill Co.; and Wyndemasters, Inc.

I also thank Marcella Hackbardt for her beautiful illustrations which, although not included in these pages, did appear in *Flyfishing Alaska.* Somehow, her name and due credit disappeared from the title page in the finished book.

Much thanks is due Bob Boyer for his photographic skills; Scott Roederer, my editor, for his encouragement, criticism, and long phone conversations when he could have been out fishing; and to all the anglers I have met astream who have freely volunteered information.

Introduction
Flies for Alaska

If you're looking for a book that contains thousands of fly patterns, you've picked up the wrong one. If you want to put together a manageable assortment of flies that will catch fish in Alaska and you don't have several years to use the trial-and-error method, you've found the right book.

Without any difficulty at all, I could have doubled or tripled the number of fly patterns described in this book. That, however, would have undermined the book's purpose. For example, there are thousands of fly patterns tied specifically for steelhead, and it may be possible to find a single volume that lists as many as 500 patterns. This is great if you're already a steelhead fanatic. You can spend hours during the off season poring over the book and randomly tying patterns that look good. But what if you've never fished for steelhead? Where do you start? Do you make a crazed attempt to tie and carry all of those patterns with you, or do you use something more scientific such as a Ouija board?

I encountered this same problem prior to my first visit to steelhead waters. Perceiving myself to be smarter than the average garden hackle, I devised a foolproof plan. I would collect all the magazines, catalogs, and books on the subject and then select only what I considered to be the best fly patterns. In theory it sounded good, but after much scrutiny and a lot of list making, I wound up with over 100 patterns that I just had to have. I didn't have the time to tie all of those patterns and buying them would have been a financial nightmare. Essentially, I was back where I started.

Instead of inundating you with hundreds of fly patterns, I have presented you with a selection of 46 flies (not including color variations) that can carry you through an entire season of fishing in Alaska. They are the patterns that I, and many other flyfishers, consistently use in Alaska.

Fly Selection Criteria

During the early stages of this book I drew up long lists of flies. The lists contained many more patterns than I wanted to offer as a realistic, manageable fly assortment, so I used a variety of criteria to pare down the selection. First and foremost, the fly had to be proven effective in Alaska. In simple terms it had to catch fish and it had to perform consistently well rather than just on that one glorious afternoon on the North Branch of Secret Creek where, if the truth be known, the fish could have been caught on just about anything misdirected into the stream including balls of lint or pieces of candy bar wrapper from my fishing vest. Although I conferred with many other flyfishers and surreptitiously pawed through their fly boxes while taking notes (or actual flies), I admit to being the sole judge and executioner.

If I haven't fished with the pattern for an appreciable amount of time, it didn't even become a candidate for inclusion here. There was no set amount of time, but looking back over the patterns presented here, the minimum use is about three seasons of fishing. This may seem harsh, and admittedly I might have left out some great new patterns. For instance, there are those two new patterns that I tried at the end of last season which impressed me so much that I have already tied a couple dozen of each pattern this winter. They could wind up to be the standards of tomorrow, in which case I'll write about them in a few years. They could, on the other hand, wind up in that stock box full of flies that I reserve to be given away to youth groups or club raffles—usually in sets of a dozen. In any case, they don't appear in this book.

Neither have I set about to fill these pages with one-of-a-kind wonder flies of my own design. I will admit to engaging in plenty of creative fly tying, but most concoctions prove to be no better than existing standard patterns. Many of my more wild attempts are fit only for the previously mentioned stock box full of flies in search of a good home. There are, though, three flies included in these pages for which I claim credit, the Bottlebrush, the Arctic Minnow, and the Katmai Slider. Stylistically they are not really new, and with the amount of fly tiers in the world I wouldn't be surprised if they have been created simultaneously by someone else. Even if that is the case, I can honestly say that I conjured up and bestowed names on these three without any other previously tied pattern in mind.

Any inferences of a scientific nature in relation to fly selection are probably after-the-fact conclusions. I may have surmised that the Olive Lake Leech is a good imitation of many of the damselflies present in Alaska's lakes, but that doesn't mean that I set out with this in mind and looked for a pattern that would imitate them. Call me an empiricist. I like to try out different patterns, and when I find one that consistently works, I have occasionally figured out—or think I have—why it works. I may tank-test some of my patterns to see if they look the way I want them to when they're in the water, but I don't scuba dive and compare my imitations to naturals or watch the reactions of fish to a particular pattern.

Don't get me wrong, though. I think matching naturals is interesting, and I enjoy reading about it and occasionally using some of the information to create one of my own patterns. However, I prefer to leave all the hard-core note taking and repetitive tests to people who enjoy that sort of activity more than I do. I will admit to having a more than casual interest in entomology (my major in college), and if I have to, I can string out and correctly pronounce some awfully impressive Latin names. It rarely seems to impress the fish though, and I reserve Latin for times when I am sitting in front of my microscope keying out some of the aquatic critters. I do this not necessarily because I think it will advance the state of my flyfishing but because I like to. Collecting and identifying aquatic insects—I am particularly fond of stoneflies—is a hobby unto itself for me.

Selecting Flies to Tie

You probably know a flyfisher who uses very few fly patterns. This flyfisher, the minimalist, may use, in varying sizes, nothing but an Adams dry fly and a Gold-Ribbed Hare's Ear nymph with good success everywhere and anytime. In contrast, there is the flyfisher who carries an amazing array of fly patterns all the time. Representing the other extreme, this flyfisher may carry a dozen different flying ant imitations among the hundreds of patterns found in his vest pockets at any one time. I'm familiar with successful flyfishers who adhere to both these extremes. Most flyfishers fall somewhere in the middle.

Extremists or those in the middle, this book is for all flyfishers. If you wish to come to Alaska with just a handful of patterns, you would be stacking the odds in your favor if you selected a chosen few from these pages. However, if you prefer to fish Alaska with a lot of patterns, you would be thoroughly prepared if you carried the 46 patterns found here. Flyfishers between those extremes—those looking for a few patterns to round out their salmon fly assortment or those figuring out which streamers to take to Alaska this year—will also find this book valuable.

Fly Tying Instructions

Although none of the patterns presented here are really difficult to tie, this book isn't designed for the beginning fly tier. You won't find instructions on how to use your whip finisher, make a dubbing loop, or spin deer hair. If you need some assistance with the basics, I would recommend getting some hands-on instruction. Books are fine once you have a base to work with, but if you're in the beginning stage, there's no substitute for sitting down, watching someone demonstrate a technique, and then trying it yourself. (I know because I am self-taught.) Fly-tying classes aren't quite at the stage where they are listed in the yellow pages, but they are more common than you might imagine. Check in at your local fly shop or sporting goods store to see if they offer a class or know of someone who does. Many individuals offer classes in their homes, and it's not uncommon to find classes offered in community school programs or at the university level where you might find a class offered in the adult or continuing education department.

As I said, I am a completely self-taught fly tier. I learned by looking at pictures of flies in the Orvis catalog and then trying to copy them as closely as possible with the materials I had. As a result, I taught myself to do quite a few things the wrong way. Well, "wrong" probably isn't the correct term. I learned to tie them differently. For example, I have not yet met another right-handed fly tier who wraps the thread counterclockwise like I do. Odds are there are some out there, but I haven't met them yet.

Of being self-taught, the part that I value most today is being able to tie a fly just by looking at a picture of it. For a long time, I assumed that everyone who tied flies could do this, but I found out that I was wrong. Some of the students in my fly-tying classes ask me to show them how to tie a fly that is similar enough to a pattern we have already done that they should be able to tie it without a step-by-step demonstration, but they can't.

That's why I have included brief tying instructions for the fly patterns in this book. And rather than assuming that you can figure out how to tie an Iliamna Pinkie but might get stumped with the mechanics of putting together a Flash Fly, there are tying instructions for all of the fly patterns. Some fly tiers may find the more complex patterns, such as the Woolhead Sculpin, difficult at first with the abbreviated instructions provided. Studying the photographs will help, as will experimentation. Most of the "difficult" patterns are just complex and often use a series of techniques you're familiar with but haven't used in the way required. Hopefully, I've given enough instructions to get most fly tiers through the steps necessary to tie all the flies in the book.

You will notice that many of the fly pattern recipes call for weight to be added to the hook. This is, of course, optional, but even if you don't typically add weight to your flies, I would strongly recommend doing so for your Alaska patterns. Even with sinking-tip lines, weighted patterns are the norm for Alaskan fishing. To be thoroughly prepared, I tie about 25% of my flies without weight.

Fly Pattern Colors

There are some practical matters that should be mentioned before going any further. One subject is color. You will see references to colors such as hot pink and fuchsia. I use these terms because these are the ones used by the supplier of the material. A problem arises when suppliers refer to the same color by different names. Aside from a manufacturer's possible proprietary notions, it's easy to see how this happens. Take, for example, one color and have three people describe it. The first may call it blue-green, the second greenish-blue, and the third aqua or jade. We all interpret colors differently. Writing about color can be biased and vague because of this.

Definitions of color from a dictionary help little. For instance,

The Random House Dictionary of the English Language describes chartreuse as "a clear, light green with a yellowish tinge." Okay, so how clear is clear? How light is the green? And how much yellow accounts for a tinge? I can't say, but if your chartreuse material happens to be a little clearer, or a little darker, or has a little more or a little less yellow than mine, I wouldn't worry about it. I think it would be a rare situation where an Alaskan fish would grab one fly and completely shun another because of a difference in hue that defied everyday description. Match your materials to the flies in the color plates and then fish them confidently. I would.

One additional note regarding color. In *Flyfishing Alaska* and past articles I have spoken of the color cerise. I have since received batches of very similarly colored materials, but they were labeled as hot pink not cerise. Further, I am told by someone who knows a whole lot more about color than I do, that cerise is more of a deep red and the stuff I have been tying with is definitely more pink than red. The solution? What I used to call cerise, I now refer to as hot pink. Now I am waiting for someone to tell me that my fuchsia is really more of a magenta, and my burnt orange really doesn't have enough burnt in it. So much for color.

Fly Pattern Categories

Flyfishers are known for putting things into discrete categories, dry flies, wet flies, nymphs, and streamers, for instance. Separating fly patterns into categories, whether to be put into a fly box or for the purpose of this book, is not a straightforward task when you take into account some of the rather unusual patterns that are used with great frequency in Alaska. For instance, in which category should we place a Ginger Bunny Fly commonly used to imitate salmon flesh? Is it a streamer? Or should it be placed under a designation of its own such as flesh flies?

Retail catalogs using standard fly pattern categories often include, almost as an afterthought, an obfuscated category called "Alaska flies" or sometimes "steelhead and Alaska flies". This could imply that flies used for steelhead or salmon and those used for grayling have enough in common to be included in the same category—a category which includes flies such as an egg pattern, a Polar Shrimp, and a mouse imitation, all from widely divergent groups. On the other hand, they definitely do not fall in line with standard categories like dry flies, nymphs, and streamers. Many things in Alaska, when compared with what people consider normal on the "outside," are a bit different.

As a result, the chapters and the fly patterns in this book are also a bit different and don't fit nicely into standard categories. For instance, the chapter titled Eggs To Flesh covers a seemingly illogical combination of flies that includes, among others, an egg pattern, a maggot fly, and a juvenile salmon imitation. If that confuses you at the outset, then you're reading the right book, and you'll begin to understand what makes flyfishing, and the flies used, in Alaska a bit different than what you might be accustomed to. To gain even more insight into the goings on of flyrodding in the 49th state, I would recommend, as modestly as possible, that you pick up a copy of my book *Flyfishing Alaska*.

Those of you that have already read *Flyfishing Alaska* may wonder why I didn't follow the same plan and describe the flies in a species-by-species chapter format. The simple answer is repetition. Take, for example, a fly such as the Egg Sucking Leech. It would have to be included as a main candidate in as many as 10 species-oriented chapters. Likewise, the flies presented in the Eggs to Flesh chapter would have to be included in chapters discussing rainbow trout, char, grayling, and to a lesser extent lake trout and cutthroat trout. Put simply, there would be too much repetition.

Alaskan trips are regularly planned to key in on one particular species of fish. As a quick reference for the angler planning to do just that, I have compiled charts that list flies in conjunction with the species for which they are most frequently used. These charts are not a final statement of a fly's worth. They are guides to get you headed in the right direction. For example, the Sockeye Orange is a great fly for sockeye salmon and that will be so noted in the appropriate chart, but that doesn't mean it will not entice the occasional rainbow, Dolly Varden, or grayling.

I also regularly meet anglers who arrive in Alaska with less than specific knowledge regarding exactly where and for what species they will spend most of their time fishing. Even though these details may be sketchy, they will at least be sure of the date of their trip, and frequently questions arise as to the best patterns to use for that time period. For that reason I have also created charts to indicate the most appropriate time periods to use the flies found within these pages. Keep in mind, though, that dates and any references to seasons have to be on the vague side unless specific locations are being discussed. The seasons in Alaska are stretched out over more than 15 degrees of latitude which, put into perspective, is similar to going from New York to Miami or from Minneapolis to Houston or from Seattle to San Diego.

Other Parts of the Country

Speaking of other locales, you will soon recognize that some of the prominent patterns found here were created in other parts of the world for fish not found anywhere near Alaskan waters. A good example is the Bomber. The Bomber was borrowed from the East Coast where they are used for Atlantic salmon. Likewise, I hope that some of the patterns discussed here may be borrowed by anglers in other parts of the country. I would highly recommend that you try some of these patterns on your home waters.

Some of these flies I had only rarely used before moving to Alaska, but once having become familiar with them I have traveled widely and found them to be good fish takers in other parts of the country and the world. For example, although its origins are in Alaska, I have used the Flash Fly with great success in waters from Belize to the Fiji Islands. Other patterns, such as an alevin—although I have not tried it extensively outside of Alaska—might be effective in any area where the flyfisher has the opportunity to fish when the post-egg stage of any game fish is present. Another natural carryover would be to use some of the patterns created for Alaska's Pacific salmon in other parts of the northwest where Pacific salmon occur or in the Great Lakes region where steelhead and other Pacific species have been introduced.

I only wish that during the several years I spent fishing in the Great Lakes region for salmon, steelhead, and trout, I had tried some of the outlandish Alaskan patterns. I'm sure that at least in a few instances the results would have been very rewarding. Equally exciting is the thought of having a pattern like the Flash Fly and being in the midst of a school of feeding bluefish along the coast of Cape Cod. I would tie one on without hesitation and fully expect a strike as I stripped it through a frenzied school.

Part of the mystique of fishing for Atlantic salmon is its cadre of honored patterns. It would be interesting to see how some of these renegade patterns from the western frontier might fare in those tradition-bound eastern waters. Can you imagine the look a guide from the maritime provinces might have on his face as you pulled out an Egg Sucking Leech and prepared to fish it? His reaction might be even stranger and more dramatic if you hooked an Atlantic salmon. It's worth a try. After all, there are many days when even venerable Atlantic salmon patterns result in no strikes. You've got nothing to lose, except possibly being laughed right off the river if it doesn't work. I, for one, will be giving some of these patterns a try during the next couple of seasons when I return to fish some Atlantic salmon waters that I haven't seen for nearly 15 years.

Equally intriguing is the thought of using a pattern like the Purple Wooly Bugger to entice the bass of the small ponds that I fished during my boyhood. The fancy lake flies, as they were called, and oversized trout patterns resulted in a few fish, but the anglers with spinning gear touting purple rubber worms always caught more and bigger fish. I fully believe that had I had a weighted Purple Wooly Bugger back then some of those bass that fell to the rubber worm would have instead attached themselves to the end of my line.

If you tie and fish the patterns in this book, you'll set yourself up for success in Alaska. Even if a trip to the Greatland isn't in your future, you may find a fly here that will work on the fish of your home waters.

Iliamna Pinkie, page 5

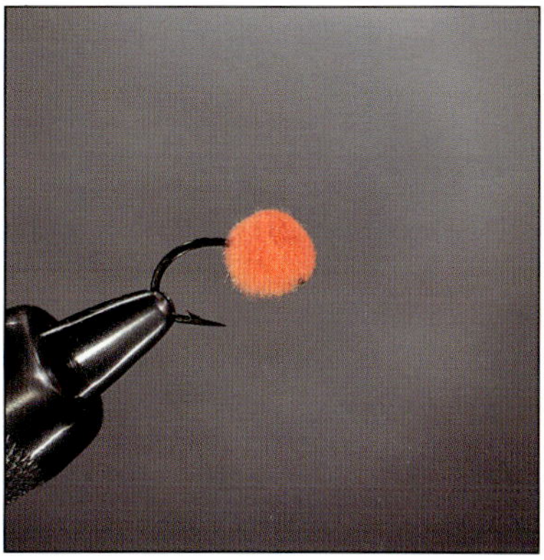

Glo-Bug, page 7

Battle Creek Special, page 8

Alevin, page 10

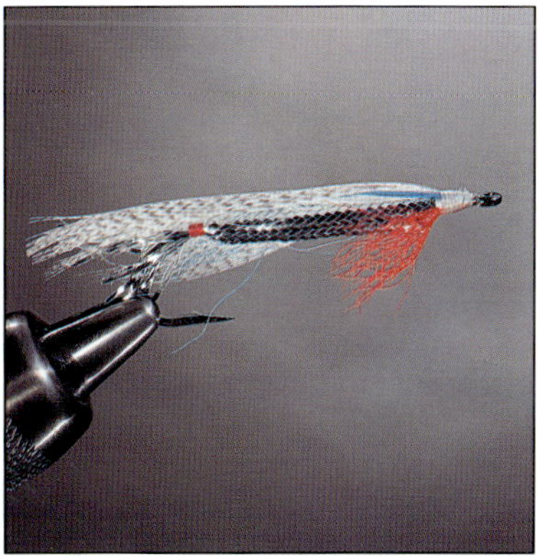

Blue Smolt, page 13

Ginger Bunny Fly, page 16

White Wooly Bugger, page 17

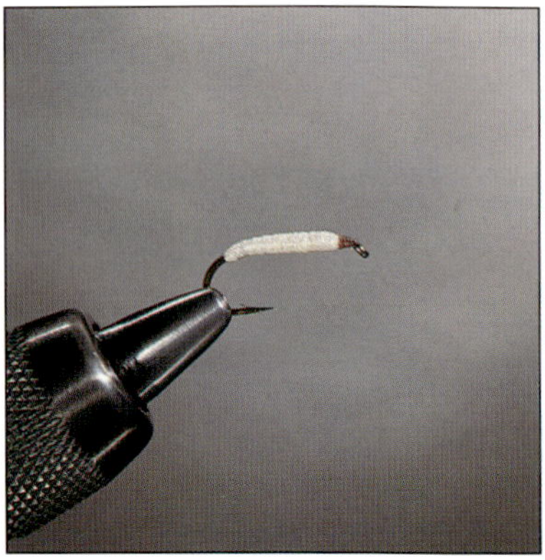

Maggot, page 19

Flash Fly, page 26

Chartreuse Everglow Fly, page 28

Hot Pink Sparkle Shrimp, page 32

Black-&-Orange Whistler, page 35

Gold Comet, page 37

Sockeye Orange, page 39

Bottlebrush, page 42

Fuschia Bunny Fly, page 45

Purple Wooly Bugger, page 52

Egg Sucking Leech, page 54

Marabou Girdle Bug, page 57

A.P. Black, page 59

Flash Body Nymph, page 61

Bitch Creek, page 65

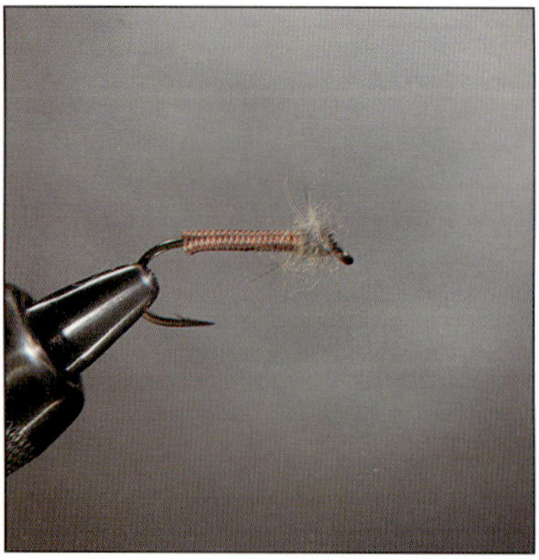

Brassie Nymph, page 68

Green Caddis Larva, page 70

Marabou Black Ghost, page 77

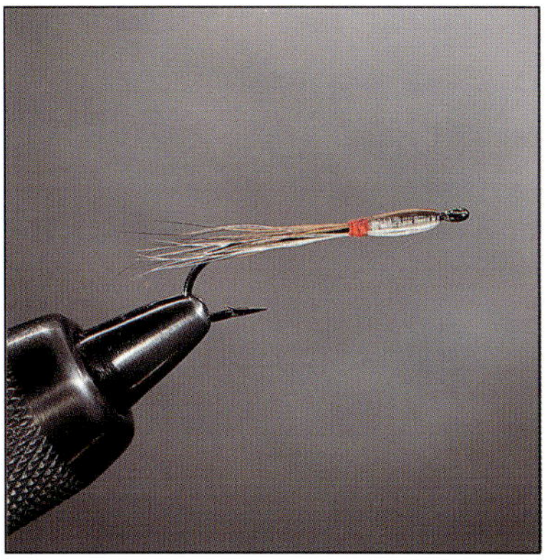

Thunder Creek, page 79

Woolhead Sculpin, page 82

Sea-Ducer, page 85

Lefty's Deceiver, page 88

Mickey Finn, page 92

Arctic Minnow, page 95

Olive Zonker, page 98

Katmai Slider, page 108

Simple Shrew, page 111

Hornberg, page 113

Blue-Winged Olive, page 116

Green Bomber, page 118

Little Yellow Stonefly, page 121

Rio Grande Trude, page 124

Humpy, page 126

Lake Leech, page 134

Pin Head Muddler, page 137

Crowe Beetle, page 139

Mosquito Larva, page 141

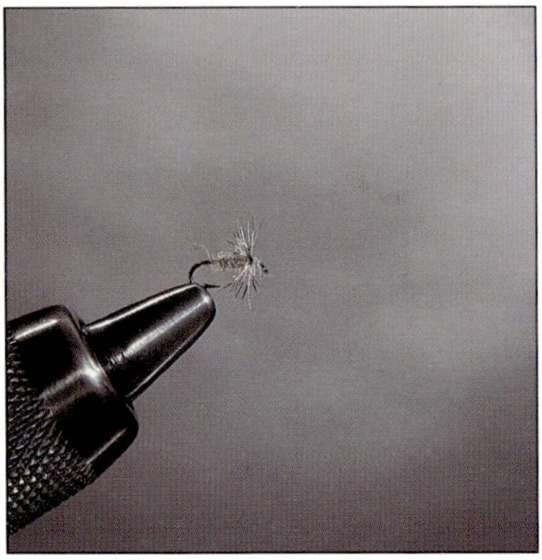

Simple Midge, page 144

Partridge-and-Yellow, page 147

Color photographs by Bob Boyer

Iliamna Pinkie, Glo-Bug, Battle Creek Special, Alevin, Blue Smolt, Ginger Bunny Fly, White Wooly Bugger, Maggot

Chapter 1
Eggs to Flesh

Some people are under the impression that the only fly they need in order to be successful in Alaska is a salmon egg pattern. On the other hand, many purists despise and refuse to fish with egg patterns, while other flyfishers outwardly agree with those sentiments but secretly carry them buried beneath some big streamers in a deep fly box. Whether you like them or not, they are often the best patterns to use. They are, however, by no means the only pattern needed in Alaska. In fact, if I had to rely on just one pattern throughout Alaska for an entire season (and I definitely wouldn't want to have to do this), I might opt for something big and ugly like a Purple Wooly Bugger.

Feelings about egg flies aside, the life cycle of Pacific salmon is extremely important to Alaska's other game fish. Simply put, salmon are the catalysts that drive many of the ecosystems in Alaska and allow species like rainbow trout to display such vigor

Char taken on egg pattern.

and to grow to tremendously large sizes. There are some river systems where salmon are not present, and consequently they have no effect on the status of any of the game fish there. The chances are good, however, that if you've seen a photograph of a very large trout or char from Alaska, it came from a drainage that supports runs of salmon. As a fisheries biologist friend of mine likes to say, "As the sockeyes go, so go the rainbows." Essentially, if sockeye runs become depressed, it will be reflected in the well-being of the rainbow trout population.

Undeniably, many species of Alaska's game fish are dependent upon salmon, but many anglers do not look beyond the salmon egg and trout relationship. They fail to recognize or give very little attention to the fact that these game fish also rely on other stages of the salmon's life cycle. Any angler who takes this fact beyond just simple recognition and uses flies that imitate these other stages will catch more fish. Using only egg patterns in Alaska would be akin to fishing a season on some great waters of the Lower Forty-Eight with only dry flies modeled to look like the large Hexagenia mayfly. Sure the Hex hatch is eagerly awaited and can be quite thrilling, but would you wander around for the rest of the season without some other flies such as Pheasant Tail Nymphs or Blue-Winged Olives? Here then, are the flies which represent Alaska's salmon smorgasbord.

Egg Patterns

Without a doubt, the most widely acclaimed fly associated with Alaska is the egg pattern. This shouldn't be surprising when you consider that salmon are found in freshwater throughout Alaska from May through November. They are there to spawn, and when a stream is filled bank to bank with spawning salmon there are enough of those little orange BBs available to other game fish that they can put on weight at a rate similar to the occupants of a southern catfish farm. There are times, especially during the early part of the salmon run, when eggs—or for that matter, anything small, round, and orange—get gobbled by wild fish with the same amount of discretion as hatchery fish display while inhaling food pellets thrown into the raceway. I'm not kidding, sometimes it's so easy there should be a law against it.

During these periods when it is ridiculously easy everyone looks like an expert. You tie on a salmon egg-colored Glo-Bug or an Iliamna Pinkie, drift it behind some spawning salmon, raise the rod tip when the line hesitates, tighten up the line, play the fish, and then repeat the procedure.

It's not always so easy though. Once these trout, char, or grayling get into the groove, they won't move very far to get an egg because they don't have to. It's similar to trout rising during a dense emergence of insects. They don't have to move to the left or right because there will be plenty of insects moving through their narrow feeding lane.

At these times your presentation of the egg pattern has to be nearly perfect. Optimally, you want your fly to drift right into the fish so that if it doesn't open its mouth the fly will hit it on the nose. If that doesn't work, you need to change the color of the egg so that it doesn't match the color of the natural. Try a shade darker or lighter than the egg you are using. In the rare instances where this also fails to work, switch to something completely different such as an A.P. Black nymph. If that also fails, try something really bizarre like a size 2 Hot Pink Sparkle Shrimp. This will usually cause the fish to do one of two things—strike or race away in fear.

Iliamna Pinkie (Chenille Egg)

This is my hands-down favorite, and I have caught more fish with it than all the other egg patterns combined. I have had mornings when an Iliamna Pinkie has accounted for more than three dozen fish. (I didn't count them, my fishing partner did). I tie 100 every season for two reasons: I give a lot away, and when I foul hook a salmon with one, which can happen quite often when you're fishing among hundreds of spawning salmon, I break off the fly. A size 8 Iliamna Pinkie hooked in the dorsal fin of a salmon won't interfere with spawning, and it would waste a heck of a lot of time trying to land a salmon on a lightweight outfit just to retrieve the fly.

Technically, an Iliamna Pinkie is nothing more than a Chenille Egg, but the name Iliamna Pinkie refers to one tied specifically with light pink chenille. There is no reason, though, why you can't tie Chenille Eggs in different colors. I have them in three main colors, light pink, light orange, and dark orange. I prefer Chenille Eggs over Glo-Bugs because I can add weight to the shank of the hook on a Chenille Egg and can't on a Glo-Bug. I would rather add weight to the fly than to the leader.

There is a fourth color, a creamy yellow, that I also carry in my fly box. It is reserved for very early and very late in the season when it works best. I have found this color to be particularly successful from mid-April until the beginning of June when fished in the vicinity of spawning grayling or suckers. Both of these fish are spring spawners and have eggs that are essentially this yellowish color. In the fall I have always presumed that the cream color represents eggs that haven't been fertilized and are covered with fungus while they are deteriorating. I can't positively say this is the reason that they work, but many times they outperform the more conventionally-colored orange eggs late in the fall, say from mid-September onward, once most of the salmon spawning has been completed.

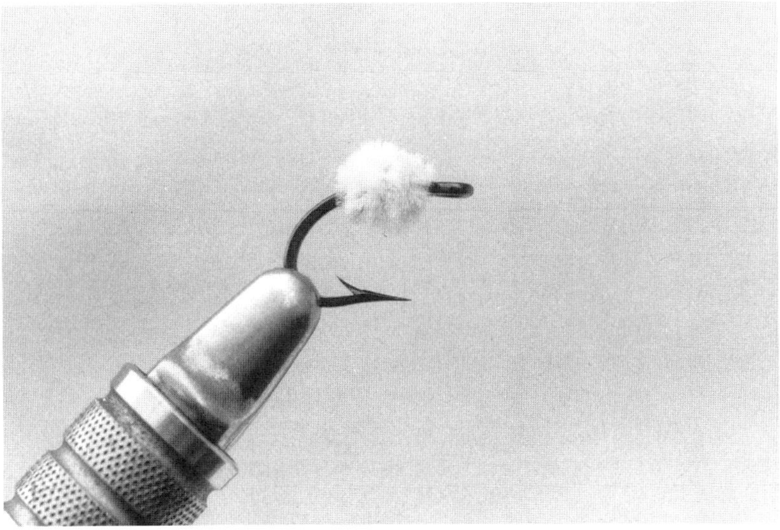

Tying the Iliamna Pinkie

HOOK:	3x short, 1x strong, e.g., Mustad #9174, sizes 6-8
WEIGHT:	.020″ lead
THREAD:	White
BODY:	Light pink chenille

1. Place three or four wraps of .020″ lead in the center of the hook shank. Secure, leaving the thread behind the lead wraps.
2. Attach the chenille and take the thread forward to the eye. Use anywhere from three to six wraps of the chenille to form a ball. Tie off and whip finish.

Glo-Bug

I don't use Glo-Bugs nearly as much as Chenille Eggs. Here, I'll have to admit, I'm in the minority. Judging from fly shop sales and glances into other flyfishers' fly boxes, Glo-Bugs are much more popular than Chenille Eggs. As I previously stated, I would rather use a Chenille Egg because I can add weight to the fly. Also, I'm not very fond of tying Glo-Bugs (maybe because I'm not too good at it).

The Glo-Bug yarn used in the construction of Glo-Bugs comes in a wide spectrum of colors from white to black. Some fly shops carry Glo-Bugs in nearly every color that's available, and they further complicate matters by adding differently colored eye spots to them. You could go crazy picking some out because there are so many colors and because some of the colors look so similar it's tough to tell them apart. I would recommend staying with the same color scheme that I outlined for Chenille Eggs: light pink, light orange, dark orange, and creamy yellow. As far as the eye spots are concerned, I'm not convinced that they make the egg any more enticing to the fish, whatever their color.

Recently a similar fly, called the Meg-O-Egg or Meg-A-Egg, has appeared on the Alaska scene. It looks much like a Glo-Bug, but the outer perimeter of the material is covered with tiny, shimmering bits of what look to be pieces of mylar. Of course, like a lot of other new patterns, it's being heralded as the greatest thing since the invention of plastic fly lines. I used them interchangeably with my other egg patterns last season and found them to be quite effective, just as their counterparts are. After only one season of use I would say that they work as well as Chenille Eggs and Glo-Bugs, but they have to go a long way before I'll say that they're any better than their predecessors.

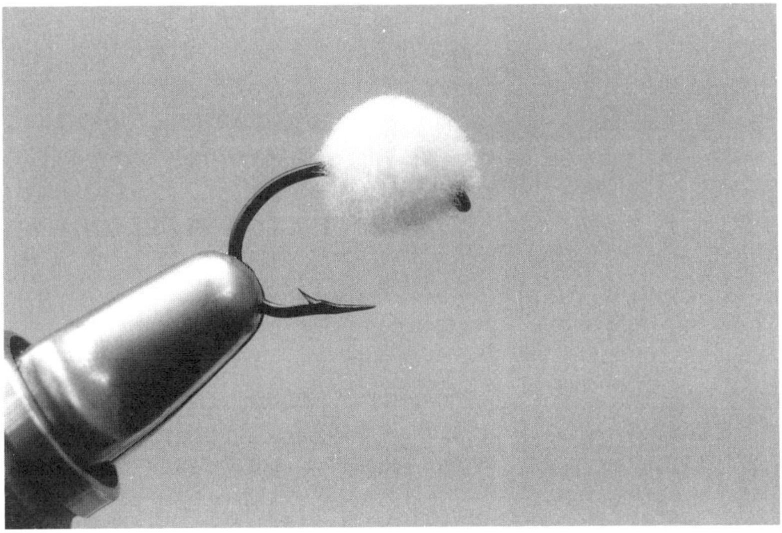

Tying the Glo-Bug

HOOK:	3x short, 1x strong, e.g., Mustad #9174, sizes 6-8
THREAD:	Pink Kevlar or other very strong thread
BODY:	Glo-Bug yarn

1. Cut pieces of Glo-Bug yarn into two-inch lengths.
2. Attach the thread to the center of the hook shank.
3. Place three pieces of yarn parallel to and on top of the hook shank and secure them, as tightly as possible, with several wraps of thread so that an equal length protrudes forward and backward from the tie-in point. Hold the yarn out of the way and whip finish.
4. Grasping the yarn at both ends, lift it straight up with as much force as possible without pulling the hook from the vise.
5. With very sharp scissors, make a single cut 1/4 inch above and parallel to the shank.

Battle Creek Special

At first glance this fly would seem to be more aptly considered an attractor pattern rather than an egg-imitating fly, but I fish it as an egg pattern and that's why I have included it here. I use the Battle Creek Special when I have to cover a lot of water. On big rivers where salmon are spawning but, because of the river's size or possibly because the water is glacially tinted, I can't see them or the trout or char that may be holding behind them, I use the Battle Creek Special. I fish the water just as I would when steelhead fishing. Rather than sight fishing to individual trout or placing the fly behind a pair of spawning salmon where I presume a trout to be, I use a series of casts while slowly wading the shoreline. In this way, I can completely cover the potential holding water. I've caught many steelhead with this fly and lots of rainbow trout that were as big as their ocean-going counterparts.

Tying the Battle Creek Special

HOOK:	3x long streamer, e.g., Mustad #9672, sizes 2-8
WEIGHT:	.030″ lead
THREAD:	White
TAIL:	White marabou
BODY:	Light pink chenille
HACKLE:	White saddle hackle, palmered, with three wraps of orange immediately behind the head

1. Wrap the hook shank with lead from directly above the hook point to two eye widths behind the eye of the hook.

2. Attach body-length marabou fibers on the top of the hook's bend for the tail.
3. Attach the chenille and saddle hackle at the base of the tail. Wrap the thread forward to the front of the lead.
4. Wrap the chenille forward and tie off.
5. Palmer the hackle forward and tie off at the same point.
6. At this same point, attach an orange hackle and make three wraps. Tie off and whip finish.

Alevins

An alevin is a salmon in the stage of its life cycle after the egg but before the juvenile fish is referred to as a fry. It is easily the least known phase of the salmon's development and consequently receives less attention than it should from flyfishers.

There are two reasons for this lack of attention. The prime season to fish an alevin pattern immediately precedes and often runs into the springtime outpouring of salmon smolt heading to the ocean. Alevins, if you are lucky enough to find one, will be somewhere in the vicinity of an inch long while an outgoing smolt may be anywhere from two to five inches in length. Since the smolt are much larger and occur in heavy concentrations that are often very visible to the angler, it's not hard to understand why the angler who may carry as many as six different smolt patterns may have never even heard of an alevin. In fact, during the early part of the spring—an excellent time of the year to use an alevin pattern—many anglers will instead use smolt-imitating flies in anticipation of what will occur a few weeks later.

Another reason for the lack of attention is the fact that alevins should remain in the gravel. They are not supposed to be found floating around among the currents of the stream. The fact that stream bottoms are continually in the process of erosion and deposition may account for why alevins are often found being swept downstream by the current, but regardless of why they are there, predators rarely pass up the chance to make a meal out of them.

This point really hit home one spring several seasons ago. Standing on the hard-packed remnants of the previous winter's snow, I spent a day of what amounted to be casting practice into the waters of the Kenai River. It was the first outing of the season and my casting which had only started out as mediocre was quickly falling into the sloppy category. Of course, the fact that I was throwing large, weighted flies didn't improve my casting and when the size 2, weighted sculpin began to fly dangerously close to my right ear, I decided it must be fairly close to quitting time. Before I left, my fly stopped in mid-retrieve, and I'm not sure who was more surprised, me or the Dolly Varden wearing a counterfeit sculpin in its lip. It was a dark fish of about two pounds, and when I restrained it to remove the fly, a pile of alevins spewed out of its mouth. How it could have found such a dense concentration of alevins to feed upon, I don't know, but since then I have never been without an alevin pattern during the early part of the season. The recipe below is the only alevin pattern that I use.

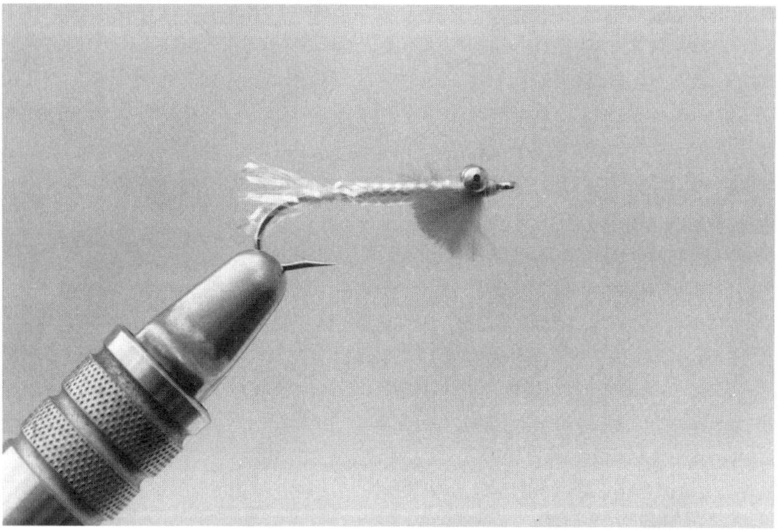

Tying the Alevin

HOOK:	4x long streamer, e.g., Tiemco #9394, sizes 6-10
WEIGHT:	.020″ lead
THREAD:	White
TAIL:	Unraveled pearl mylar tubing
BODY:	Pearl mylar tubing
THROAT:	Orange marabou tied in a short tuft
EYES:	3mm bead chain

1. Cover the rear two-thirds of the hook shank with lead. Secure, leaving the thread in the tail position.
2. Slide a section of mylar tubing over the hook shank so that the unraveled portion extends past the thread and slightly beyond the bend of the hook. Secure the mylar with several wraps of the thread and whip finish.
3. Reattach the thread just behind the eye of the hook. Secure the front end of the mylar tubing.
4. Secure a pair of bead chain eyes to the hook shank using a figure-eight wrap.
5. Attach a short tuft of marabou directly underneath the bead chain eyes. Tie off and whip finish.

Smolt

No doubt that you've heard, as someone knots a streamer to a leader, comments about big fish eating small fish. Most of the time, though, the angler who resorts to the streamer is just one step away from defeat. Even though most anglers carry at least a few streamer patterns, those anglers are not what you would call streamer aficionados. Not, at least, in the same way that you would refer to someone as being a nympher or a dry fly purist.

No, there are not too many flyfishers out there who specialize in streamer fishing. Instead a streamer or baitfish pattern is typically used when there are no risers to cast to, whatever hatch should be occurring doesn't seem to be developing, or it's too late or too early in the season for much of anything to be going on. A streamer is the type of fly often used when you've given up but still want to continue fishing. They are often fished half-heartedly and used in what would be considered poor conditions.

When you take these things into consideration, it makes it even more astounding to think of how many big fish really do fall for a streamer. I've often wondered how many flyfishers would become streamer devotees if they took the time to fish their baitfish patterns during the best fishing periods and through the best water. Taking this a step further, imagine there was a regular event similar to the salmonfly hatch in Montana, only make the organisms coming downstream small fish instead of insects—talk about a feeding frenzy!

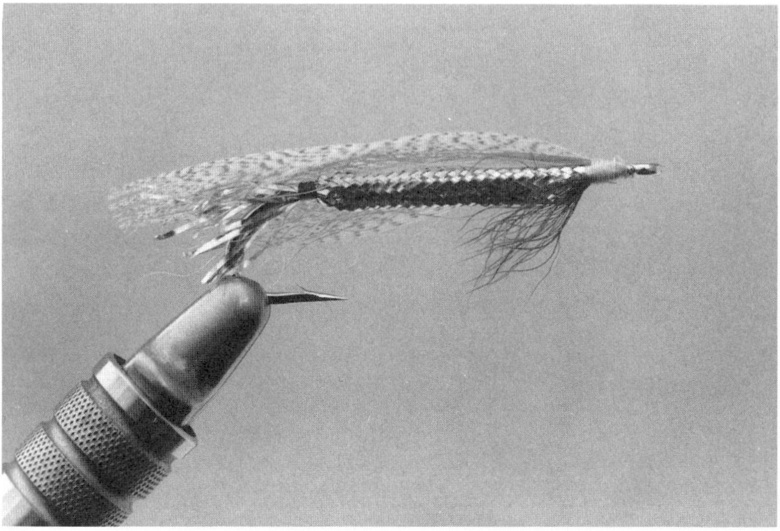

Well, imagine no more. That very event occurs every year in Alaska with a regularity that is much more dependable than your average insect emergence. Every spring millions of juvenile salmon called smolt migrate downstream to the ocean, and the trout and char which have just spent the winter months in a state of near torpor respond by gorging themselves on these bright little fish.

There have been hundreds of patterns created to imitate these smolt, and I have tried a whole bunch of them. However, I always go back to using the Blue Smolt. It's made of common materials, it's easy to tie, and it rarely fails to interest fish that are feeding on smolt. Due to a variety of natural factors, smolt vary in size so I tie the Blue Smolt in a wide array of sizes. I used to substitute the blue calf tail with different colors, but none seem to work as well as the blue, so I now carry just the blue.

One of the reasons that I believe the fly to be so effective is the way the mallard overwing is tied flat over the back as opposed to using two feathers and matching them side to side as is done on a traditional streamer. The flat surface of the mallard feather causes it to wobble and plane differently than a traditional streamer, and this undoubtedly has something to do with its attractiveness.

Tying the Blue Smolt

HOOK:	4x long streamer, e.g., Tiemco #9394, sizes 2-8
WEIGHT:	.030" lead
THREAD:	Red and white
TAIL:	Unraveled silver mylar tubing
BODY:	Silver mylar tubing
THROAT:	Red calf tail
UNDERWING:	Blue over white calf tail
OVERWING:	Single mallard flank feather laid flat

1. Cover the hook shank with lead from directly above the hook point to a distance of two eye-widths behind the eye of the hook. Secure with red thread, leaving it at the tail position.
2. Slip a section of mylar tubing over the hook shank so that the unraveled end extends past the thread and slightly beyond the hook's bend. Secure the mylar with several wraps of red thread and whip finish.
3. Attach the white thread just behind the eye of the hook and secure the front end of the mylar.
4. Attach a clump of white calf tail fibers and then a clump of blue calf tail fibers creating a bi-colored streamer wing.
5. Tie in a shorter clump (twice the gap width in length) of red calf tail in the throat position.
6. Tie in a single mallard flank feather (or similar feather) so that it lies flat on top of the hair wing. Whip finish.

Flesh Flies

As true as the progression of the seasons, Pacific salmon return to the streams of their origin each year to undertake their act of procreation. Once finished, they die. I mention this only because every season I meet an amazing number of visiting anglers who do not know this and express shock and bewilderment when they visit a stream that is clogged with dead salmon. They lament that it seems to be such a waste, which of course is exactly what it isn't. The salmon's biological strategy is different than that of steelhead or Atlantic salmon both of which may spawn more than once in their lifetime. Pacific salmon instead put all of their energy into one event. Why it takes place in this fashion is about as simple or complex as why some flowers sprout, blossom, and perish in one season leaving only their seeds, while others survive to bloom for several more seasons.

At first glance, especially to the angler who enjoys catching fish, it would seem to make more sense if these fish survived to spawn a second time. What they do by dying, though, is far more important than what would happen if they made their way back to the ocean and returned to spawn in subsequent years. The carcasses of these spawned-out fish become part of the complex food web of the streams they spawn in, and it is no small part that they play. In an indirect way they even become food for their own progeny, which is one of the most outstanding forms of altruism in the animal world. The bacterial organisms that may begin to invade their bodies even before they die become the basis for the food chain that supports everything from macroinvertebrates such as mayflies, stoneflies, and caddisflies to higher organisms such as mink, bald eagles, and bears.

Flyfishers, however, do not have to understand all the intricacies whereby spawned-out salmon essentially become the fertilizer for the stream ecosystem. Instead they only have to be aware of just one thing—given the opportunity, many game fish will feed on the flesh of these dead salmon. This does not mean that you have to tie an imitation the size of an adult salmon. Instead, you need to imitate the small pieces of flesh that break loose and float downstream as the salmon decays.

The conditions in which flesh flies will work are easily identifiable. Obviously, you want to fish them where there is a run of salmon. The flies may work at almost any time once the salmon have arrived, but the best action really doesn't begin to occur until near the very end of the spawn. Depending upon the species of salmon and the location of the drainage, this may typically be any time from the end of July through September and even later. Flesh flies will continue to be good producers for weeks after the fish have stopped spawning.

Within the stream look for obstructions that snag whole carcasses as they float downstream. It's not unusual to find spots where hundreds of salmon carcasses have collected, and when you do, fish a flesh pattern just downstream from them as you would fish an egg pattern downstream from a redd. The results are usually outstanding. In fact, many people with whom I have fished have taken their largest rainbows on flesh flies. Ditto for char.

Ginger Bunny Fly

If your criteria for a great fly include ease of tying, inexpensive and readily available materials, and the ability to make trout fight over the fly, the Ginger Bunny Fly has to be in the running for number one.

The first time I used a Ginger Bunny was a memorable experience. I had sloshed out through the tail end of a back water eddy and was about to make my first cast out to the seam between the slow and the fast water when a raft appeared just upstream from me. The rafters were staying fairly close to the bank I had waded out from, and as a result they didn't see me until it looked as though a collision was imminent. A shout brought them to their senses, and they swung into the shallow back eddy. After paddling furiously and making a big commotion, they finally broke loose from the dead water and drifted downstream. This back eddy was a depository for salmon carcasses, and along with stirring up the bottom muck, I think they hit every dead salmon with their paddles. As water muddied with debris, whole dead salmon, and many more parts of decaying carcasses floated by me, I was quietly progressing from slightly perturbed to mildly enraged. Then I saw the fish.

Almost at my feet was a big fish, and within moments I noticed that there were fish all around me. Whether they had been there all the time or not I don't know, but I could see them now and they were moving back and forth in the current and gorging themselves on hunks of salmon. They were hitting the pieces with such force that small particles would break off, and it reminded me of sharks hitting those dead mackerel that divers stick through bars on their diving cages. I tied on a Ginger Bunny Fly, dropped it into the water and watched a fish slam into it. That ended the show at my feet because I had to wade to shore to land the fish, but the fishing continued. Before I left that spot I landed several rainbows, none small. The biggest was 27 inches long and shaped like the Goodyear blimp. Needless to say, I don't want to be anywhere near a dead salmon unless I have a Ginger Bunny Fly with me.

Tying the Ginger Bunny Fly

HOOK:	3x long streamer, e.g., Mustad #9672, sizes 2-6
WEIGHT:	.035″ lead wire
THREAD:	White
TAIL:	Short section of ginger rabbit strip
BODY:	Ginger rabbit strip wound forward from bend to eye of hook

1. Cover the hook shank with lead from a point directly above the hook point to a distance of two eye-widths behind the eye. Secure, leaving the thread at the tail position.
2. Attach a section of rabbit strip at the tail position leaving a shank-length portion extending beyond the bend as a tail. Take the thread forward to the eye. Wrap the remaining rabbit strip forward to the thread, tie off, and whip finish.

White Wooly Bugger

The other flesh flies that I carry and consistently catch fish with are a White Bunny Fly and a White Wooly Bugger. I tie the two Bunny Flies in sizes 2–6 because the length of most rabbit hair and the thickness of the tanned skin makes it difficult to use on smaller hooks. There are times, such as when I am after fish that probably won't exceed a couple of pounds, when I like to use a four- or five-weight fly rod. Casting a size 4, soaking-wet Bunny Fly on a four-weight isn't much fun, so that's when I use the White Wooly Bugger. Using a smaller amount of marabou for the tail and proportionally smaller hackle and chenille, I can tie Wooly Buggers in sizes 6-10 to use with lighter weight outfits.

Tying the White Wooly Bugger

HOOK:	3x long streamer, e.g., Mustad #9672, sizes 6-10
WEIGHT:	.025" lead wire
THREAD:	White
TAIL:	White marabou
BODY:	White chenille
HACKLE:	White saddle hackle, palmered the length of the body

1. Cover the hook shank with lead from a point directly above the hook point to a distance of two eye-widths behind the eye. Secure, leaving the thread at the tail position.
2. Tie in a tail of marabou fibers approximately equal to the length of the shank.
3. Attach the chenille and saddle hackle at the tail position. Wrap the thread forward to just behind the hook eye.
4. Wrap the chenille forward to the thread and tie off. Palmer the hackle forward to the same point. Tie off and whip finish.

Maggot

To some people the flesh fly is about as unpleasant a concept as they have encountered in the realm of fly tying. If you are one of these people and you get queasy just thinking about decaying salmon flesh, the Maggot will make your stomach do flip-flops. Obviously a maggot isn't part of the salmon's life cycle, but its presence and availability as fish food are dependent upon salmon to such a degree that it warrants inclusion in this chapter.

Picture a small to medium-sized salmon stream filled with pairs of salmon hovering over spawning redds. In the ensuing weeks these salmon will die. The salmon carcasses which do not get caught on underwater obstructions or get washed into deep pools will lay scattered along gentle, sloping stream banks and gravel bars. Here they become forage for many species of birds, mammals, insects, and in the case of those that do slough off into the water, fish. Frequented by insects which lay eggs, the carcasses that don't wash away become infested with a writhing mass of maggots.

There are several ways that these maggots can find their way into the stream, but the two most common are rising water levels brought about by rain and the beach-rinsing action of the rain itself. Regardless of how they get there, trout, char, and grayling gobble them up with the same enthusiasm that a bluegill exhibits when presented with a nightcrawler.

The maggot does not need to be presented bouncing along the bottom, but I find that weighting the fly does help to get it down closer to the fish in fast moving water. In slower water I use an unweighted maggot. Even though the pattern is tied with poly yarn, which does not absorb water, there is no hackle to support the fly on the surface, so it will sink slowly and allow you to control the depth of the fly by varying your presentation and the length of your leader.

As you may have guessed by now, you don't have to be aware of the water temperature, barometric pressure, or any Latin names to recognize when it's time to try a maggot pattern. If it is the appropriate time, telltale signs will be littered along the banks and gravel bars of the river you're fishing.

If you're a little bit uncertain whether you want fellow anglers to know that you're carrying a fly that imitates a maggot, don't worry—you can pass it off as a caddis larva.

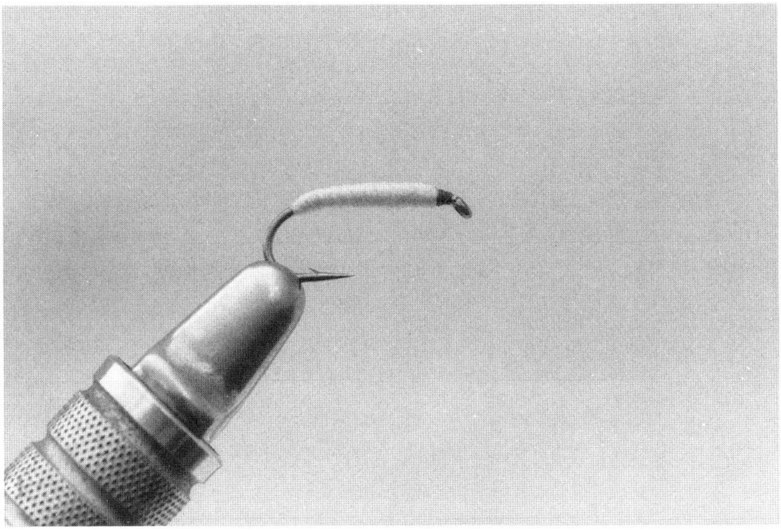

Tying the Maggot

HOOK:	2x strong wet fly, e.g., Tiemco #3769, size 10
WEIGHT:	.020" lead
THREAD:	Brown
BODY:	Cream poly yarn

1. Cover the hook shank with lead from a point directly above the hook point to a distance two eye-widths behind the eye. Secure, leaving the thread at the tail position.
2. Attach the poly yarn and wrap the thread forward to a point just behind the eye. Wrap the poly yarn to the thread and tie off. Form a head with the tying thread and whip finish.

Chapter 1: Eggs To Flesh
Fly and Season

	JAN	FEB	MAR	APR	MAY	JUN	JUL	AUG	SEP	OCT	NOV	DEC
Iliamna Pinkie, light pink						X	XXX	XXX	XXX			
Iliamna Pinkie, light orange						X	XXX	XXX	XXX			
Iliamna Pinkie, dark orange						X	XXX	XXX	XXX			
Iliamna Pinkie, cream				XX	XXX	X			XX	XXX	X	
Glo-Bug, light pink						X	XXX	XXX	XXX			
Glo-Bug, light orange						X	XXX	XXX	XXX			
Glo-Bug, dark orange						X	XXX	XXX	XXX			
Glo-Bug, cream				XX	XXX	X			XX	XXX	X	
Battle Creek Special				XXX	XXX	XXX	XXX	XXX	XXX	XXX	X	
Alevin				XXX	XXX							
Blue Smolt					XX	XXX	X					
Ginger Bunny Fly							X	XXX	XXX	XX		
White Bunny Fly							X	XXX	XXX	XX		
White Wooly Bugger							X	XXX	XXX	XX		
Maggot								XXX	XX			

Chapter 1: Eggs To Flesh
Fly and Species

	KS	RS	CS	PS	SS	RT	ST	CT	CH	LT	AG	NP	SF
Iliamna Pinkie, light pink						X	X	X	X	X	X		
Iliamna Pinkie, light orange						X	X	X	X	X	X		
Iliamna Pinkie, dark orange						X	X	X	X	X	X		
Iliamna Pinkie, cream						X	X		X		X		
Glo-Bug, light pink						X	X	X	X	X	X		
Glo-Bug, light orange						X	X	X	X	X	X		
Glo-Bug, dark orange						X	X	X	X	X	X		
Glo-Bug, cream						X	X		X		X		
Battle Creek Special					X	X	X	X	X	X	X		
Alevin						X		X	X		X		
Blue Smolt						X		X	X	X	X	X	X
Ginger Bunny Fly						X			X	X	X		
White Bunny Fly						X			X	X	X		
White Wooly Bugger						X		X	X	X	X		
Maggot						X			X		X		

KS = King Salmon, RS = Red or Sockeye Salmon, CS = Chum Salmon, PS = Pink Salmon, SS = Silver or Coho Salmon, RT = Rainbow Trout, ST = Steelhead, CT = Cutthroat Trout, CH = Arctic Char/Dolly Varden, LT = Lake Trout, AG = Arctic Grayling, NP - Northern Pike, SF = Sheefish

Flash Fly, Everglow Fly, Sparkle Shrimp, Whistler, Gold Comet, Sockeye Orange, Bottlebrush, Fuchsia Bunny Fly

Chapter 2
Flash And Fluorescence

In this chapter you will find the creations that, often without regard for rhyme or reason, entice Pacific salmon—and sometimes other species—into striking. If you're regularly frustrated with flies the size of Tricos, you're going to have a ball with these flies.

Most of them are so big that you can use a half spool of rod winding thread on them and still come out with a neat looking head. The materials are typically so bright that, unlike that small bit of dubbing which can become lost on the table right in front of you, you'll never have to look twice to find them. In fact, tiny bits of hot orange, bright pink, and fluorescent chartreuse chenille along with silvery strips of Flashabou have a way of showing up on the living room carpet long after you've put your tying stuff away and the guests have arrived.

Some of this stuff even glows in the dark, and in a pinch most of these flies make better than average Christmas tree ornaments.

Sparkle Shrimp and chum salmon.

Beyond attracting fish and being seasonal decoration, if you're really daring and need to jazz up your fashion statement, you could—as I have seen on more than a couple of occasions—wear them as earrings.

Before you read on I would like to point out that although you might assume all of these flies are strictly for salmon, you shouldn't overlook them when fishing for other species. This applies specifically to the angler in search of steelhead, but many of these patterns have also resulted in red letter days for other trout and char. On the flip side, there are many other patterns scattered throughout other chapters that can be used for salmon. In both cases the crossover will be noted in the text concerning the fly, and additional information can be gleaned from the tables following each chapter.

You will find flies that are suitable for use in saltwater in this chapter. For more details and a list of saltwater fly patterns see Appendix A.

You will notice that many of the fly patterns in this chapter are tied in a wide range of hook sizes. This is to accommodate the tremendous range of the size of fish for which they are used. For example, the same fly pattern may be used for both king salmon and pink salmon, and while kings may reach weights of 70, 80, or even 90 pounds, the average pink will likely be closer to three or four pounds. Obviously you might not want to use the same size hook for king and pink salmon. You could catch a pink on a 3/0 hook and a king on a size 8 hook, but if you are tying one of these patterns for a specific species, it does make sense to use an appropriately sized hook. The following table lists my recommendations for doing just that.

King Salmon	4/0-1
Sockeye Salmon	6-10
Pink Salmon	4-8
Chum Salmon	1/0-4
Silver Salmon	1/0-4
Steelhead	1/0-6

Flash Fly

I know some anglers who are experts when it comes to catching salmon with a fly rod, and more than one of them will tell you that they could get through an entire season of salmon fishing with just a Flash Fly. That's high praise indeed when you take into account the often fickle nature of Alaska's salmon. I wouldn't want to be salmon fishing with just one fly pattern, but I wouldn't disagree with these anglers. If I was relegated to using only one fly for salmon, it would have to be the Flash Fly. Here's why.

Most anadromous fish, whether silver salmon or sea-run Dolly Varden, will at some time in their life cycle feed on other fish—quick little silver things that reflect a flash of light when they are feeding, being chased by predators, or simply moving fast. If you are a determined imitationist, you could identify all the important species of baitfish, find out which will be most prevalent in the area you are fishing, and then tie a fly that matches the subtle combination of white, green, blue, and silver hues of the fish.

The Flash Fly, however, is ideally suited to imitate whatever small fish happens to be swimming around. The concept—whether it was premeditated or not—is simple. The Flash Fly does not try to imitate the subtle coloring of a live fish, instead it mimics the flash that is seen when a silvery fish moves quickly.

Because of the nature of small fish constantly being pursued by predators, the Flash Fly is best fished in a nervous, darting, erratic manner. A variety of inconsistent stripping motions ranging from short, quick strips to long, steady pulls will usually result in some awfully hard strikes, regardless of the species of fish doing the striking. I'm not sure why, but maybe the predator is conditioned to knock the scales off the prey on the first hit so that it will not get away. In any case, I have never had any fish take a Flash Fly gently.

As you would expect, the Flash Fly is an excellent choice when you're fishing in an area where the fish will have just returned from the sea or in the saltwater itself. Do not, however, give up on the Flash Fly once you have moved away from coastal areas, because king, silver, chum, and pink salmon still show an interest in the fly long after they have left the salt. It's not just a salmon fly either. The Flash Fly has accounted for quite a few steelhead, char, cutthroat trout, and some offbeat species not particularly well known by the flyfisher, such as flounder and rockfish.

The original silver and red pattern has been changed by many fly tiers, and now Flash Flies exist in almost every available color of Flashabou and Poly Flash. The most popular colors are silver and orange, silver and pink, and purple. I have used almost all of them at one time or another, but I still rely most heavily on the silver and red original.

If you want a fly that can be used almost anywhere and that draws explosive strikes from salmon, you want a Flash Fly.

Tying the Flash Fly

HOOK:	Saltwater or salmon wet fly, e.g., Mustad #34007 or #3407, sizes 3/0-6
WEIGHT:	.035″ lead
THREAD:	Red
TAIL:	Silver Flashabou
BODY:	Silver Poly Flash
UNDERWING:	Red calf tail or bucktail
OVERWING:	Silver Flashabou
HACKLE:	Red saddle hackle

1. Cover the hook shank with lead from directly above the hook point to a point two eye-widths from the eye of the hook. Attach the thread and secure the lead, leaving the thread at the wing position.
2. Attach a wing-length section of Flashabou projecting forward beyond the eye of the hook. On top of that, attach a wing-length section of calf tail. Work the thread back to the tail position.
3. Tie in the tail of Flashabou and attach three strands of Poly Flash. Take the thread forward to the wing tie-in position. Wind the Poly Flash forward to the thread and tie off.

4. Attach the the hackle, make three or four turns, and tie off.
5. Now fold the calf tail and the Flashabou backward to a typical wing position and overwrap it with thread to hold it there. Cover the remaining material to form a head. Whip finish. (This procedure is known as the reverse-winging technique. By locking in the wing fibers, it makes it much less likely that they will be pulled out. I use it for almost all of my standard-winged steelhead and salmon flies.)

Everglow Fly

The Everglow Fly is made of material that may cause you to step back and gasp when you see it hanging on the fly shop wall. You might, on the other hand, walk by it passing it off as a fad that belongs in the same category as wearing neon-colored clothing. I admit I initially had the latter attitude. I wasn't particularly interested in a fly that glows in the dark, nor did I see a big reason for needing one.

That was in late June, and fresh in my mind was the four weeks I had just spent in Prince William Sound. The last night I had hiked around an island taking pictures from dinner until breakfast, and it never got dark. So I guess I wasn't receptive to a fly material that used darkness as a component of its effectiveness. However, like everyone else, I took my turn stepping into a dark closet to watch the glow emanating from the packages of pink, chartreuse, orange, and white Everglow material. I'd come into the fly shop with the intention of buying just a few spools of thread, but it didn't seem right to leave with such a small bag, so I grabbed several packages of the Everglow stuff more out of impulse than any real desire to tie flies with it.

The flies I tied with the material impressed me as much as the material had, but I'll give any fly at least as few tries. I hadn't planned on doing much salmon fishing at night so I stashed them away in a back-up box. I subsequently loaned the box to a first-time flyfisher who accompanied me on a silver salmon fishing trip later that summer. On the first day of that trip, after he released his third silver to my none, I waded down to him to make sure he didn't have any more questions about this difficult sport of flyfishing. There were fish porpoising around both of us, and I wanted to find out what he was using. An orange-and-white Everglow pattern was attached to his tippet. I felt a little bit foolish having to borrow flies from him.

Those Everglow patterns were the only patterns in my back-up box that I didn't also have in my regular salmon box. As you might expect, I moved back upstream and proceeded to catch some silvers. That experience was enough for me to begin carrying a variety of Everglow patterns and trying them under different conditions. That was several years ago, and I still use Everglow Flies for silver salmon and, even more so, for king salmon.

The Chartreuse Everglow Fly has been a steady producer of king salmon for at least five years. It is one of the first patterns I reach for when I am rigging up my 10-weight for kings. I fish it deep on a fast sinking-tip line or sinking shooting head, running it through the deep holes where kings hold. I use a standard wet-fly swing and then finish up with a moderately fast retrieve in foot-long strips. Strikes—anything from a slight hesitation to an outright wallop—may occur at any time. This same chartreuse version is also one of the patterns that I rely heavily upon when fishing for silver salmon in saltwater.

The other Everglow pattern that I use has a white body and orange wing. It is an excellent fly to start with if you encounter discolored water while you're fishing for silver salmon. It's also a good pattern to use in clear water conditions when, on rare occasions, the silvers refuse a Flash Fly. In either case it is best fished deep with a dead drift swing and then strip retrieved at the end of the swing.

Tying the Chartreuse Everglow Fly

HOOK:	Saltwater or salmon wet fly, e.g., Mustad #34007 or #3407, sizes 3/0-4
WEIGHT:	.035" lead
THREAD:	Chartreuse
UNDERBODY:	Light-colored chenille, floss, or yarn to cover lead
TAIL:	Unraveled chartreuse Everglow tubing
BODY:	Chartreuse Everglow tubing
UNDERWING:	Chartreuse calf tail or bucktail
OVERWING:	Chartreuse Everglow winging material
HACKLE:	Chartreuse saddle hackle

1. Cover the hook shank with lead from a spot directly above the hook point to a spot two eye-widths behind the eye. Secure, leaving the thread at the tail position.
2. Place a section of Everglow tubing over the hook shank letting the unraveled end protrude past the thread and slightly beyond the hook shank. Secure with several wraps of thread and whip finish.
3. Reattach the thread just behind the eye of the hook and secure the front part of the tubing. Create a wing of bucktail and Everglow winging material using the reverse-wing method previously described for the Flash Fly. (Remember that because the wing will be stroked backward after being tied forward, the wing materials will need to be tied in the opposite sequence that you want them to appear in the finished wing. Therefore, tie the Everglow material first and then put the bucktail fibers on top of that. When the wing is reversed the Everglow will be on top with the bucktail underneath it.)
4. Attach the saddle hackle and make three or four wraps. Pull the wing fibers into the wing position, secure with thread, and then cover the remaining material to form a head. Whip finish.

Orange-and-White Everglow Fly

HOOK:	Saltwater or salmon wet fly, e.g., Mustad #34007 or #3407, sizes 3/0-4
WEIGHT:	.035″ lead
THREAD:	Bright orange
UNDERBODY:	Light-colored chenille, floss, or yarn to cover lead
TAIL:	Unraveled white Everglow tubing
BODY:	White Everglow tubing
UNDERWING:	White calf tail or bucktail
OVERWING:	Orange Everglow winging material
HACKLE:	Orange saddle hackle

Sparkle Shrimp

I don't know if real shrimp sparkle, and I wouldn't even begin to tell you that this pattern looks like a shrimp—it doesn't to me. What the fish make of it, I'm not sure. It probably wouldn't matter if I did know because I label the fly an attractor pattern and fish it as one. I first tied and tried this fly in 1985 after I noticed it in *Fly Fishing for Pacific Salmon*, and I have been using it in several different colors since then. The first ones that I used were either chartreuse or hot pink, and they worked so well that I immediately tied others in all kinds of colors from black to white. Since that time I have weeded out many of the colors, and I now carry just four—black, hot pink, chartreuse, and orange.

Although I have caught four species of salmon (no sockeye yet) and steelhead on all of the colors, there are times when specific colors seem to produce the best. As a general rule the Chartreuse Sparkle Shrimp and the Hot Pink Sparkle Shrimp are most attractive to chum salmon, and the orange version is best for kings and pinks. The Hot Pink Sparkle Shrimp is usually the one preferred by silver salmon. It is also the best all around color for any salmon or steelhead. The Black Sparkle Shrimp is the least productive of the four colors, but it often turns up a salmon-sized rainbow trout when I am fishing it in waters that contain both salmon and rainbows. This happens enough that I carry several of them in my box of oversized nymphs that I use to prospect for rainbows in big water. Lately the Black Sparkle Shrimp has also been turning up some nice steelhead, and as a result I am using it more and more when fishing for them. It's something that I would recommend you give a try even if your steelhead waters do not fall within the confines of Alaska.

Sparkle Shrimp are almost always most effective when fished dead drift, but I still strip retrieve them for a short distance before I pick up for the next cast. Silver and pink salmon will occasionally smash this fly during the strips, but kings, chums, and steelhead rarely do, preferring the Sparkle Shrimp with a dead drift or swinging presentation.

The dressing below is for the Hot Pink Sparkle Shrimp. The other colors are tied by replacing the chenille, hackle, and the thread with the appropriate color. As with most salmon and steelhead patterns, I recommend that you weight the majority of these flies and reserve just a few to be unweighted.

Tying the Hot Pink Sparkle Shrimp

HOOK:	Salmon wet fly, e.g., Mustad #36890, sizes 1/0-6
WEIGHT:	.035″ lead
THREAD:	Hot pink
TAIL:	Pearl Flashabou
BODY:	Hot pink chenille
HACKLE:	Hot pink saddle hackle
SHELLBACK:	Pearl Flashabou

1. Weight the hook shank from a spot directly above the hook point to a spot two eye-widths behind the eye. Secure, leaving the thread in the tail position.
2. Tie in a clump of Flashabou for the tail and leave tag end material extending forward far enough to be placed over the top of the fly and tied off at the head later. Tie in the chenille and the saddle hackle at the tail position. Take the thread forward.
3. Wrap the chenille forward and tie off at the head of the fly. Palmer the saddle hackle over the length of the body and tie off at the head.
4. Bring the leftover Flashabou over the top of the body, creating a shellback, and tie off. Form a head with thread and whip finish.

Black-and-Orange Whistler

An Everglow Fly or a Flash Fly tied on 1/0 hook is an awfully big fly by most flyfisher's standards, but when you find yourself staring into the water at a dozen kings that range anywhere from 25 to 50 pounds, all of a sudden those flies don't look so big. Maybe that's exactly how the fish feel too, because there are times when the standard patterns don't seem to interest them at all. Whenever this happens I resort to a Black-and-Orange Whistler. Tied on a hook equal in size to other patterns, the Whistler presents a much bigger offering, and sometimes that's exactly what king salmon want. For example, an Everglow Fly tied on a 3/0 hook will be rather slim and will essentially be as long as the hook—approximately one-and-a-half inches. A Whistler tied on the same hook is a big fluffy affair that totals somewhere closer to four inches in length.

Who first decided to cast this saltwater pattern into a freshwater river in Alaska and why they decided to do it remain a mystery to me and everyone whom I have asked. I first became familiar with it

Whistler and Everglow Fly.

as a king salmon fly about seven years ago. Willing to try anything, I used it for the first time on the Deshka, a river in the upper Cook Inlet drainage, when the kings weren't responding to any of the flies that I was throwing at them. Whether it was the color—I have very few other black salmon flies—or the size, I am not sure, but it did change the attitude of those fish. In response they smashed into the fly on every fourth or fifth cast. The following day I fished it for hours without so much as a bump, and when I switched back to more typical salmon flies like a Flash Fly or an Everglow Fly, I began to get strikes. Why the change? I have no idea.

That first day that I used the Whistler for king salmon earned it a spot in my salmon box at least for that season. Due to its subsequent performance it has been a staple for me whenever I am after kings. It still exhibits great variation in its day-to-day effectiveness, but the days when it does work almost always coincide with a period when more typical salmon flies don't. It has never, at least for me, proven effective for other species of salmon, but it has surprised me with some chunky rainbow trout that were holding close to the kings.

I weight all of my Whistlers and tie them full to a length of about four inches. For additional weight you could substitute lead eyes for the big bead chain eyes, but then you would miss the excitement of hearing this fly whistle past your ear, which may be why Dan Blanton (the originator of this pattern) named it the Whistler. Whistlers come in many different colors, but the only one that I have had success with for king salmon is the black-and-orange variety described below. I have begun to experiment with a white-and-orange dressing, which so far looks promising.

As with any other fly used for king salmon, the best presentation will be dictated by the mood of the fish. Often they will pick it up while it is dead drifting or just as it begins to pick up speed on the downstream swing. Most of the time, though, the Whistler is at its best after it has completed its swing and hangs in the current. Sometimes the fish will hit the fly after it has hung in the current for almost a minute without any movement. If hanging the fly doesn't bring about any response, slowly strip it in and you may be greeted with a vicious strike. It's during this very slow strip retrieve that the kings really belt this fly. I guarantee this will startle you even if you are paying attention.

Tying the Black-and-Orange Whistler

HOOK:	Saltwater or salmon wet fly, e.g., Mustad #34007 or #3407, sizes 3/0-1/0
WEIGHT:	.035″ lead
THREAD:	Bright orange
BODY:	Black bucktail tied in at staggered positions along the shank of the hook and extending well beyond the bend of the hook
WING:	Eight black saddle hackles
TOPPING:	Ten strands of peacock herl
HACKLE:	A full collar of orange marabou
EYES:	5mm bead chain

1. Weight the hook shank from a spot directly above the hook point to a spot two eye-widths behind the eye of the hook. Secure, leaving the thread in the tail position.
2. Attach a tail of bucktail at least the length of the hook shank. Two-thirds up the hook shank attach another bunch of bucktail so that it extends as far back as the tail fibers. Attach three more clumps of bucktail, two on the sides of the hook shank and one in the throat position, all extending back as far as the tail fibers.

3. Attach eight saddle hackles in the wing position, four on each side, splayed outward.
4. Attach a topping of 10 peacock herls.
5. Attach a collar of marabou.
6. Immediately in front of the marabou tie in a pair of bead chain eyes, cover the butt sections of the marabou with thread, and whip finish.

Gold Comet (Sockeye Variation)

Not an Alaskan creation by any means, the Gold Comet and the Comet patterns in general are widely recognized as a staple in the assortments of flies used by steelhead anglers in the Pacific Northwest. The Gold Comet is also used for steelhead in Alaskan waters and, as it is typically tied, it is also a proven pattern regularly carried by anglers who are pursuing anything from king to pink salmon. My main reason for including it here, though, is to highlight its effectiveness for sockeye salmon, considered by many flyfishers to be the most finicky of all Alaska's salmon.

You may notice that the Gold Comet pictured here is tied very sparse in comparison to the representatives of this pattern which are found in fly shops or shown in catalogs. The very sparse dressing is the key to its success as a sockeye fly. The oval tinsel and thick tail of calf tail or bucktail fibers of the traditionally tied pattern have been replaced with flat gold mylar tinsel and ginger hackle fibers. Overall, this presents a much more slim and trim profile. Unlike most Comets you're likely to see, it is best tied in sizes 6-10. Using sparse dressings and small sizes is the way to be successful when fishing for sockeyes.

This small, sparsely-dressed Gold Comet has been a consistent producer since I first fished for sockeyes with it many seasons ago. Some people have theorized that a fly like this may represent any one of a number of small organisms such as amphipods, euphausids, or shrimp larvae that sockeye salmon feed on while they're in saltwater. Whether this assumption is correct and why they take them while they're in freshwater, I cannot say for sure, but the fly does work well.

Technique is as important as fly pattern when fishing for sockeye salmon. Dead drift, however you accomplish it, is the best tactic, and the fly must be presented at the same level in the water column that the fish are holding. Sockeyes may move from side to side to intercept a fly, but they will rarely move up or down to do the same.

As previously mentioned, the Gold Comet is not only a sockeye fly. Tied as large as size 1/0 it has accounted for more than just a few king salmon, and in sizes 2 and 4 it is also used for silver and pink salmon as well as steelhead. When used other than for sockeyes, however, it is best to incorporate a larger bunch of bucktail for the tail and considerably more hackle to create a fuller dressing. The larger patterns for king salmon also frequently use additional weight on the hook shank and even substitute lead eyes for the bead chain eyes.

Tying the Gold Comet (Sockeye Variation)

HOOK:	Salmon wet fly, e.g., Mustad #36890, sizes 6-10
THREAD:	White
TAIL:	Ginger hackle fibers
BODY:	Flat gold tinsel
HACKLE:	Ginger
EYES:	3mm bead chain

1. Attach the thread at the tail position and tie in a sparse hackle fiber tail.

2. Attach gold tinsel and take the thread forward to the head position. Wind the tinsel forward to the head and tie off, creating the body.
3. Attach bead chain eyes and then attach a hackle directly behind them.
4. Take three or four turns of hackle and tie off. Wrap the thread ahead of the bead chain eyes and whip finish.

Sockeye Orange

The Sockeye Orange has the distinction of being one of the few flies tied expressly for use as a sockeye salmon fly. More often than not, flies used for sockeyes are patterns, or variations thereof, created for other salmon or, more commonly, steelhead. The Sockeye Orange was originated sometime around 1985 by Mike Mercer of Redding, California. He has fished in Alaska extensively. Its sparse design is typical of sockeye patterns, and it is most commonly tied on a size 8 hook.

My first experience with the Sockeye Orange occurred on a stream in the Iliamna area when an angler gave me a couple of the flies. He called them "Sockeye Oranges", and as he promised, they did work very well on the sockeyes in that area during the next week. Over the next several years I collected many Sockeye Orange patterns, and most of them were very different than that first Sockeye Orange that I'd been given. Currently, I have a collection of almost two dozen Sockeye Orange patterns. Some have more green, black, or white in them than orange, but they are all tied very sparse on small (sizes 6-10) hooks. It has gotten to the point where I think that to some anglers the Sockeye Orange denotes a type of fly rather than a specific pattern. Although I haven't tried all of them extensively, I don't doubt that they will all work to some degree.

The original dressing as described by Mike Mercer included a wing of dyed black squirrel tail and hot orange saddle hackle attached with black tying thread. There is no body or tail, and originally it was tied on a size 8 or 10 Eagle Claw #1197 nickel-plated hook. Currently Mercer uses a Tiemco #9394 hook in the same sizes.

The dressing I have described below is slightly different from the original, but it is the one that I have used for many seasons and can emphatically say works. Although I have taken a few pink salmon with it, I use it almost exclusively for sockeye salmon and fish it in the same manner as that previously mentioned for the Gold Comet.

When the sockeyes arrive in June and July, the Sockeye Orange is one fly that I am never without.

Tying the Sockeye Orange

HOOK:	Salmon wet fly, e.g., Mustad #36890, sizes 6-10
THREAD:	Black
BODY:	Flat silver tinsel
HACKLE:	Orange
WING:	Black calf tail or squirrel tail

1. Attach the tinsel and take the thread forward to the head position. Wind the tinsel forward to form a smooth body. Tie off.
2. Attach the wing (using the reverse-wing method). Attach the hackle and make three turns. Tie off.
3. Stroke the wing fibers back into position, secure with the thread, and whip finish.

Bottlebrush

As unlikely as it may seem, there is at least one big advantage to living in an area, Anchorage, Alaska, for instance, where winter weather makes any flyfishing impossible—you have lots of time to tie flies. Now I don't want to imply that the winter weather in Anchorage is any more severe than some locales in states like Montana, Minnesota, or Maine, but there is one thing you can count on up here. Regardless of the winter's severity, it lasts a long time. Long enough, unless you take too many vacations to warmer climates, that you can tie all the flies you intend to use during the following fishing season. One winter I had all my fly boxes filled by mid-February. This long winter was indirectly responsible for the creation of the Bottlebrush.

I am very task minded when I sit down at my tying vise. Usually I work off a list of all the flies and their sizes that I would like to have for the coming season. Once this list is completed I become creative and tie all kinds of what some of my friends kindly refer to as experimental patterns. It could be a function of the length of the tying season, or the length—and darkness—of the winter, I am not sure, but eventually I make the leap from what can be considered creativeness to craziness. It's usually a lot of fun, but typically the resultant flies do nothing more than frighten fish and make fellow anglers laugh. The Bottlebrush was the result of one of these crazed tying sessions.

Because I tie and fish a lot of Gray Ghosts, I got tired of buying small packets of silver pheasant feathers (used for the shoulder). So, I bought a whole silver pheasant skin. To get the shoulders on the Ghosts the appropriate size I routinely pull away some of the fibers from the base of the stem, and I used some of these scraps lying on my tying bench for throat hackle on Polar Shrimp-type patterns. On the next try I used a whole, small body feather and wound it as a wet fly-style hackle collar, and finally I tied a fly with a silver pheasant body feather palmered along the chenille body. The dressing was so full that I left off the wing. At the time the fly looked so interesting that I tied six or seven of them.

I went through almost the entire following season without fishing the fly (it no longer looked so interesting) until one day late in October on the Anchor River. It was on a weekend, and the river had quite a few other steelhead anglers on the water. This one particular guy kept cutting in below me before I could finish fishing a stretch of water. He did it several times in one morning and at one point he actually waded into a pool within several feet of a steelhead that at that moment was attached to my line. When I released the fish, he waded upstream to me—instead of walking along the bank—and rather than politely asking, he demanded to see what kind of "lure" I was using. Fortunately, I had just snipped off the Egg Sucking Leech that I was using because it had been gnawed beyond recognition, and I took one of those Bottlebrushes from my box and handed it to him. I left him with that fly and headed downstream to have some lunch and hopefully lose him for the rest of the day.

About midafternoon he found me again. He waded right into the stream to interrogate me. The fly was stuck in his baseball cap, and with his fingers locked up in its gills, he held a still wet female steelhead with lines of blood seeping down its sides. Somewhere, I thought, some deity who watches over steelhead anglers was getting back at me for having lied to this guy and not giving him an Egg Sucking Leech. According to him the fly worked great, and he wanted to know what it was called and where he could get some more. By the way he acted I am sure he thought I was lying when I told him he probably couldn't buy them anywhere because I had just made up the pattern last winter and didn't even have a name for it.

I would like to say that I tied a Bottlebrush on at that moment and proceeded to catch a steelhead, but it didn't work that way. I completed the rest of the weekend without so much as a bump from a steelhead, and I used the Bottlebrush quite a bit. A week later on a Kodiak Island stream it accounted for two steelhead and many more char. The following season it consistently encouraged salmon to strike, resulted in a few wonderful days of steelheading, and even fooled a few rainbow trout. Now it is firmly entrenched among my top 10 salmon and steelhead patterns (which is why it is included here).

I usually turn to the Bottlebrush when the fish, whether salmon or steelhead, seem responsive to a fly that is being stripped rather than dead drifted. The Bottlebrush has taken fish while being dead drifted, or at the apex of a typical wet fly-style swing, but it always seems to work best at the end of a drift when I strip it back in foot long bursts. Although I tie it in both weighted and unweighted versions, my entire supply of Bottlebrushes is tied on size 4 hooks, except for a small number of 1/0's which I reserve for king salmon.

Tying the Bottlebrush

HOOK:	Salmon wet fly, e.g., Mustad #36890, sizes 1/0-4
WEIGHT:	.035″ lead
THREAD:	White
TAIL:	Hot pink hackle fibers
BODY:	Hot pink chenille
HACKLE:	Silver pheasant body feather, palmered over the front third of the body

1. Weight the hook shank from a spot directly above the hook point to a spot two eye-widths behind the eye. Secure, leaving the thread at the tail position.
2. Attach a tail of hackle fibers.
3. Attach the chenille and take the thread forward. Wrap the chenille forward covering the rear two-thirds of the shank. Secure but do not cut the remaining chenille. At this point tie in the pheasant body feather by the tip end.

4. Wind the thread forward to the head position. Wrap the chenille to the thread and tie off.
5. Now palmer the pheasant feather forward to the head and tie off. Whip finish.

Fuchsia Bunny Fly

I know that we have already covered the Bunny Fly (Chapter 1: Eggs To Flesh), and you may be thinking that it's such a simple pattern why bring it up again. Well, if you think a Bunny Fly is a Bunny Fly is a Bunny Fly, you're wrong. Put a size 2, bright fuchsia-colored Bunny Fly in your hand, and there's no way either you or the fish are going to confuse it with the Ginger Bunny Fly that is used to imitate flesh. They are used for completely different purposes and different species.

Essentially, the Ginger Bunny Fly is used to imitate salmon flesh and catch species such as trout, grayling, and char, while the Fuchsia Bunny Fly imitates absolutely nothing. It's an attractor pattern and is used to catch salmon. I know I am setting myself up for an argument here because there are people, including myself, who have caught salmon on a Ginger Bunny Fly and trout and char on a fuchsia one. But even so, I once caught a chum salmon on a yellow bass popper, and although it may happen again, I don't think I would ever put the yellow bass popper on a list of flies for chum salmon.

A bright pink Bunny Fly was, and still is, regarded by some as an effective salmon fly, but the color of the Fuchsia Bunny Fly makes its predecessor look as somber as a muted earth tone, and its ability to entice salmon into striking surpasses the old pink bunny to the same degree. Over the past couple of years this has been a must-have pattern for silver salmon, but I've done equally well with it on chums, pinks, kings, and steelhead.

I have always thought that one index of how good a fly is, is the number of variations or near-identical replicas of the fly that spring up around it. Lately, I have seen variations of the Fuchsia Bunny Fly with everything from white saddle hackles to unrav-

eled silver mylar tubing attached to them. I can't say that any of that additional material has made the fly better or worse. I try the new varieties on occasion, but for now I continue to place my faith in an unadorned Fuchsia Bunny Fly.

Because the rabbit fur pulsates with the slightest breath of current underwater, it can be effectively fished without any additional action imparted to it. King salmon, as well as chums, pinks, and silvers, will often pick it up as it tumbles along the bottom. However, don't overlook the strip retrieve or twitches while it drifts downstream; these tactics can often be deadly. The strip retrieve, in particular, may cause a chum or silver salmon to race up and hit the fly so hard that you'll overreact and break your tippet by striking too hard.

With this pattern I don't fool around with a bunch of different sizes. I tie almost all of them, weighted, on size 2 hooks which can be cast reasonably well on an eight-weight, the rod I usually use when salmon fishing. I do use a larger outfit when I'm specifically fishing for king salmon, but I continue to use the same size Bunny Flies. The rabbit fur soaks up a lot of water causing the fly to be heavy when you're casting it. This, in addition to the weight added to get the fly to swing deep, makes very large sizes such as 1/0 or 3/0 seem like casting bricks, so I stick with the size 2.

Tying the Fuchsia Bunny Fly

HOOK:	3x long streamer, e.g., Mustad #9672, size 2
WEIGHT:	.035″ lead
THREAD:	Fuchsia
TAIL:	Short section of fuchsia rabbit strip
BODY:	Fuchsia rabbit strip wound in tight spirals along the entire hook shank

1. Weight the hook shank from a point directly above the hook point to a spot two eye-widths behind the eye. Secure, leaving the thread at the tail position.
2. Tie in the rabbit strip leaving a shank-length portion extending beyond the bend for a tail. Take the thread forward.
3. Wrap the remaining rabbit strip forward in tight spirals to the head position. Tie off and whip finish.

Chapter 2: Flash And Fluorescence
Fly and Season

	JAN	FEB	MAR	APR	MAY	JUN	JUL	AUG	SEP	OCT	NOV	DEC
Flash Fly					X	XXX	XXX	XXX	X			
Everglow Fly, chartreuse					X	XXX	X	XXX				
Everglow Fly, orange/white							XX	XXX	XXX	XX		
Sparkle Shrimp, black						XXX			XXX	X		
Sparkle Shrimp, hot pink				XX	XXX	XXX	XXX	XXX	XXX	XX		
Sparkle Shrimp, chartreuse							XX	XX				
Sparkle Shrimp, orange					X	XXX	XXX	XXX	XXX	X		
Whistler, black/orange					X	XXX	X					
Gold Comet				X	XX	XX	XX					
Sockeye Orange						XX	XX					
Bottlebrush					X	XXX	X		XXX	XXX	X	
Fuchsia Bunny Fly					X	XXX	XXX	XXX	XXX			

Chapter 2: Flash And Fluorescence
Fly and Species

	KS	RS	CS	PS	SS	RT	ST	CT	CH	LT	AG	NP	SF
Flash Fly	X		X	X	X		X	X	X			X	X
Everglow Fly, chartreuse	X				X								
Everglow Fly, orange/white					X		X						
Sparkle Shrimp, black						X	X						
Sparkle Shrimp, hot pink	X		X	X	X		X		X				
Sparkle Shrimp, chartreuse			X	X									
Sparkle Shrimp, orange	X		X	X	X		X		X				
Whistler, black/orange	X												X
Gold Comet		X						X					
Sockeye Orange		X											
Bottlebrush	X						X		X				
Fuchsia Bunny Fly	X		X	X	X								

KS = King Salmon, RS = Red or Sockeye Salmon, CS = Chum Salmon, PS = Pink Salmon, SS = Silver or Coho Salmon, RT = Rainbow Trout, ST = Steelhead, CT = Cutthroat Trout, CH = Arctic Char/Dolly Varden, LT = Lake Trout, AG = Arctic Grayling, NP - Northern Pike, SF = Sheefish

Wooly Bugger, Egg Sucking Leech, Marabou Girdle Bug, A.P. Black, Flash Body Nymph, Bitch Creek, Brassie Nymph, Green Caddis Larva

Chapter 3
Subsurface Uglies

As you've already learned, you can use all kinds of flies for Alaska's game fish. Egg patterns behind spawning salmon are standard fare; gaudy attractors fill out the menu for salmon. Streamers are almost always a good bet, and dry flies, as you'll read later on, are much more effective than they are reputed to be.

However, when it comes time to answer the question of what flies to use and how to fish them to catch the most fish, the best answer is often four words: big, ugly, and deep. In Alaska, this means the following. With a total disregard for the tradition of the sport and an equal disdain for any flyfishing delicacy, rig up with your fastest rated sinking-tip line, attach a three-foot section of monofilament for the leader, and tie on a big, ugly fly—preferably on a size 2 or 4, 3x long hook that has its shank heavily wrapped with lead. Describing the casting style needed to deliver this offering to the fish is beyond the scope of my work here. Let's just say that you probably don't want to do it with your heirloom bamboo rod.

Not every one of the flies presented in this chapter is big and ugly—there a few smaller ones that actually imitate aquatic insects. There are even times when these smaller flies can be successfully presented with a floating line. There are, however, many Alaskan flyrodders who, if they were writing this chapter, would simply list seven different colors of Wooly Buggers (including, of course, the Egg Sucking Leech which could be considered nothing more than an aberrant Wooly Bugger). Then they might throw in something smaller, such as a size 4 Bitch Creek Nymph, for their eighth pick.

A selection like that would definitely account for a lot of fish, but you are awarded very few points for style, grace, or ability when fishing those flies. Essentially what you do is get the Wooly Bugger into the water and when you feel a tug on the line, tug back. If it's a rock, break off and tie on another Wooly Bugger. If it's a fish, great. Floating an A.P. Black just under the surface film might work even

Rainbow caught on subsurface fly.

better, but then you would have to pay attention to things like drag and slight hesitations of your line and leader—things which require concentration—if you wanted to catch any fish.

Now, I'm not turning my nose up at Wooly Buggers. I use them quite a bit and catch a lot of fish with them every season. And you probably could fish entirely with Wooly Buggers and do quite well, but if you did, you would miss out on some other really interesting fishing.

Wooly Bugger

It would be difficult—maybe impossible—to come up with a fly pattern that is more universally accepted and used by flyfishers in Alaska than the Wooly Bugger. From its beginnings as a counterfeit cranefly larva, it is now used to imitate a wide variety of things and as an attractor pattern. It spawned the ever-popular Egg Sucking Leech and probably many other variations. Darker patterns may imitate a leech or a sculpin, and white may be taken as a piece of salmon flesh. Some of the bright, multi-colored Wooly Buggers imitate nothing at all, but they all have one thing in common—they catch fish. If I had to, I would venture to guess that more Alaskan game fish are caught on a Wooly Bugger than any other pattern. I know of at least one angler who visited Alaska with a fly assortment consisting of nothing but Wooly Buggers. Not surprisingly, he caught a lot of fish.

I could go on and on about Wooly Buggers, because the variations are limited only by the imagination of the fly tier and the available colors of chenille, saddle hackle, and marabou (a subject which in itself is staggering). The limits don't stop there either, because anglers frequently weave two colors of chenille together to create the body. With some sense of practicality in mind and after several years of fishing with many different colors of Wooly Buggers, I have settled on just two (besides the flesh fly version), a purple and a chartreuse-and-black. I have caught more species of Alaskan fish on a Purple Wooly Bugger than on any other fly, and the chartreuse-and-black version is one of my standards for steelhead and big rainbow trout. Other popular colors are black, brown, and olive.

How good is a Purple Wooly Bugger? Every off-season I make sure that I have three or four dozen tied up to begin the season. Last year I had depleted my stock by mid-June. Consequently, I found myself sitting on a high bank above a remote river tying Purple Wooly Buggers. We were midway through a float trip, and both Doug Kennemer and I had exhausted our supplies of them. Hordes of mosquitoes swarmed us, but we had decided to sit still until we had tied at least a couple of dozen, the bare minimum to get us through the rest of the trip. The mosquitoes had a field day, but we finished. When the plane arrived to pick us up several days later, only a couple of well-used Purple Wooly Buggers remained in our vests. Some of the flies were lost to snags, but most were simply chewed beyond recognition by voracious rainbow trout. If there is any maxim that applies to Purple Wooly Buggers, it would be, you can never have enough of them.

I rank the Chartreuse-and-Black Wooly Bugger right behind the Purple Wooly Bugger in effectiveness. It has two main qualities which make it attractive to fish. The marabou tail offers good movement in the water, and the contrast set up by the two colors makes it quite visible. I've caught everything from salmon to grayling on it, and it has often interested steelhead when it seems as though nothing else will. As a steelhead fly, it has become one of my standards, and I wouldn't consider going on a steelhead fishing trip in or out of Alaska without one.

Wooly Buggers can be fished in lakes and rivers throughout the season in Alaska. They are usually fished dead drift and then allowed to swing as the line bellies in the current and begins to drag the fly. Once the swing has completed, it's best to retrieve the fly using a variety of speeds. Strikes may come at any time. In fact, about the only time you can say with any assurance that you won't get a strike is when the Wooly Bugger is not in the water.

All species of freshwater game fish in Alaska, with the possible exception of sockeye salmon, are susceptible to a Wooly Bugger. Make sure you have some.

Tying the Purple Wooly Bugger

HOOK:	3x long streamer, e.g., Mustad #9672, sizes 2-10
WEIGHT:	.035″ lead
THREAD:	Black
TAIL:	Purple marabou
BODY:	Purple chenille
HACKLE:	Purple saddle hackle, palmered

1. Wrap the hook shank with lead from a spot directly above the hook shank to a spot two eye-widths behind the eye of the hook. Secure, leaving the thread in the tail position.
2. Tie in a shank-length section of marabou for a tail. At the same point, attach the chenille and the saddle hackle. Take the thread forward to the eye of the hook.
3. Wrap the chenille forward to the thread and tie off.
4. Palmer the hackle over the body. Tie off and whip finish.

Chartreuse-and-Black Wooly Bugger

HOOK:	3x long streamer, e.g., Mustad #9672, sizes 2-10
WEIGHT:	.035″ lead
THREAD:	Black
TAIL:	Black marabou
BODY:	Chartreuse chenille
HACKLE:	Black

Egg Sucking Leech

Any fly that is this ugly and makes no attempt to disguise its ugliness with a pretty name has to be good.

I wrote a magazine article several years ago which highlighted Alaska's most popular flies, and after interviewing anglers, tackle shop employees, guides, and lodge staff, the Egg Sucking Leech turned out to be, overall, the most popular pattern. Because so many flyfishers tie their own flies, numbers are difficult to pin down, but the last commercial fly tying order that I filled was for somewhere in excess of 200 dozen Egg Sucking Leeches. If this is any indication, the Egg Sucking Leech may still be Alaska's most popular fly. Even though I have given up the drudgery of commercial fly tying, I still tie many Egg Suckers for myself each season.

Essentially, this fly is nothing more than a Purple Wooly Bugger with enough space left at its head to tie in a lump of pink chenille. The first ones that I saw were black, not purple. However, anglers prefer Purple Wooly Buggers over black, and it didn't take long for the standard Egg Sucking Leech to become purple. As with many patterns that have been around for a while and are successful, it is now tied in many color variations. None seem to work as well as the pink and purple combination.

I do have to clear up what could possibly become another one of those great Alaskan myths. I recently read a flyfishing book by an English author who included the Egg Sucking Leech among his featured patterns. In the text he mentions that it is widely used in Alaska, and then he goes on to say that it imitates the leeches which hold behind spawning salmon and latch onto free-floating eggs that drift downstream. Huh? If you can picture a school of leeches quietly undulating in the current behind spawning salmon, your imagination has got mine beat. To my knowledge (and I have asked nearly everyone I know who has fished with an Egg Sucking Leech), no one has yet seen a leech swimming around with a salmon egg attached to its oral sucker.

Now, I don't doubt that some leeches, especially those types that are known to be scavengers, would feed on salmon eggs while they are moving around the substrate, but the Egg Sucking Leech has nothing to do with that. It is simply the combination of two very effective patterns, a single egg and a Purple Wooly Bugger.

They were combined with the idea that two great patterns put together would equal one that was as good or even better—and it did. Despite the name, it was not intended to imitate a leech attached to an egg. Egg Sucking Leech is simply a colorful name.

I figured it was my duty to clear this up before it got out of hand, like a lot of other Alaskan stories. I can hear it now. "Yup, there we were fishing egg patterns behind some spawners when a school (a school?) of those killer leeches swam into the area. Those suckers will go right through your neoprenes if you're not careful. Thank God, we had a .357 magnum with us..." Well, I think you get the point.

To put it succinctly, the Egg Sucking Leech is a necessity when fishing in Alaska. Not having this pattern would be like going on a five-day backpacking trip without your backpack. You might get where you're going, but you won't have what you need once you get there.

Tying the Egg Sucking Leech

HOOK:	3x long streamer, e.g., Mustad #9672, sizes 2-10
WEIGHT:	.035" lead
THREAD:	Black
TAIL:	Purple marabou
BODY:	Purple chenille

HACKLE:	Purple saddle hackle, palmered
HEAD:	Pink chenille wound to form the shape of an egg

1. Weight the hook shank from directly above the point of the hook to a spot three eye-widths behind the eye of the hook. Secure, leaving the thread at the tail position.
2. Tie in a shank-length piece of marabou for the tail. At this same point, attach the purple chenille and the saddle hackle. Take the thread forward to the front of the lead, leaving room for the chenille head.
3. Wrap the purple chenille forward and tie off.
4. Palmer the saddle hackle along the length of the chenille body and tie off.
5. Attach the pink chenille and with three to five wraps, form a ball. Tie off and whip finish.

Marabou Girdle Bug

It is not uncommon for fly tiers to take an already good fly and try to make it even better. Often the changes don't make the fly any more enticing to fish than the original already is. This variation of the Girdle Bug, however, is an exception, at least in Alaska. The Girdle Bug is a good fly. The Marabou Girdle Bug is a great fly.

One August day I found a large school of silver salmon resting in a deep pool in the canyon section of a river. Even though the water was very deep, they were holding high enough up in the water column that they were clearly visible. An occasional one or two would playfully porpoise out of the water. Thinking that I was in for a fish-in-a-barrel type of situation I chose a Flash Fly and was greeted by a hard strike on the first cast. I could only land the fish on the short rock ledge I was standing on, so it took quite a while before I finally tailed the eight-pound silver and then released it.

The commotion that that silver had caused didn't move the remaining fish up or downstream, but it did cause them to hold much deeper. Repeated casts with the Flash Fly brought no response, and even after I rested the pool for quite some time, the fish stayed deep and refused to take any standard silver salmon patterns that I showed them. Desperation lead to attempts with all kinds of patterns until a Marabou Girdle Bug made its second deep swing through the pool. I connected with a big silver and then later another and another. The Marabou Girdle Bug changed what might have been just another day to a memorable one of frenzied activity. The silvers rarely let the fly swing through more than two or three times without a strike.

On an October day on a very remote and relatively unfished stream I managed to hook a steelhead with a Marabou Girdle Bug. Besides a deep, dogged fight, the steelhead managed to make three long sizzling runs and catapulted itself completely out of the water three times. That one fish would have easily made for a wonderful day, but on the next cast from the same spot I hooked a second steelhead that fought like it was trying to outdo the first. I will admit that some remote Alaskan steelhead waters offer steelheading that is, at least in terms of the numbers of fish caught, comparable to no other waters. This, however, was the first time I had landed two steelhead on two successive casts. Three casts later, and having moved only six or seven steps downstream, I hooked and landed a third. Incredibly, five casts had yielded three steelhead.

I could go on and cite many more successful exploits with the Marabou Girdle Bug. It simply is one of those big ugly patterns that fish love.

Although it usually results in spectacular catches, I typically reserve the Marabou Girdle Bug for special situations. I weight it extra-heavy and use it where chutes of fast water dump into pools or where swift streams enter lakes. Trying to get a fly down to fish that may be holding in those kinds of water is usually difficult, and that's when I pull out this heavily-weighted, fast-sinking fly. Regardless of the fish species that may be holding there, it is almost always the best fly to use in that situation. In particular, it's a fantastic fly for rainbow trout and lake trout, and it has accounted for some of the largest grayling I've ever seen.

Weighting it heavily as I do, it's not the most pleasant fly in the world to cast, and its entry into the water is usually about as delicate as throwing a rock in the water. Add that to the fact that on the ugly scale it ranks right up there with the best and that it looks like something tied by an inept beginning fly tier, and you have a fly that at first glance does not have any appeal whatsoever to the average flyfisher. If, however, you overlook these shortcomings and fish with it, you'll probably agree with me when I say that this fly should come accompanied with a written guarantee of its effectiveness.

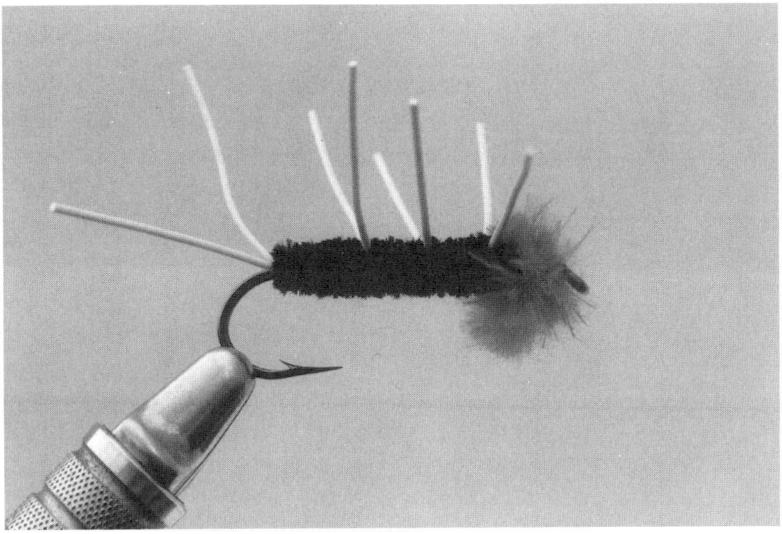

Tying the Marabou Girdle Bug

HOOK:	3x long streamer, e.g., Mustad #9672, sizes 2-6
WEIGHT:	.030″ lead flattened and overwrapped with flat lead
THREAD:	Black
TAIL:	White rubber strips
BODY:	Black chenille
LEGS:	Three sets of white rubber strips
COLLAR:	Short orange marabou

1. Wrap the hook shank with lead from a spot directly above the hook point to a spot three eye-widths behind the eye. Secure with thread and then flatten the lead with pliers. Overwrap with flat lead (Twist-Ons or LED lead).
2. Attach the three sets of rubber legs, spacing them evenly along the hook shank.

3. Attach two rubber strips for the tail and tie in the chenille at the same point. Take the thread forward to the front of the lead.
4. Wind the chenille forward being careful to wrap closely behind and in front of each set of rubber legs. Tie off.
5. Add a collar of marabou. Tie off and whip finish.

A.P. Black

Flyfishing literature often refers to flyfishers in terms such as dry-fly purists or dyed-in-the-wool nymph anglers. If I had to be pigeonholed, I could be included in the latter category. I rely heavily on nymphs. I always have and I probably always will. When I started flyfishing, I used them in pursuit of everything from bass-pond bluegills to small stream brook trout to the largest of brown trout. Upon arriving in Alaska I continued my use of nymphs and was pleased to find that they are just as deadly on fish here as they are throughout the rest of the country.

I carry many nymphs, but when I reach for my nymph box in Alaska, nine times out of 10 I am intent on selecting an A.P. Black. There are other predominantly black nymphs that I could select, but because of great results during many seasons, I prefer the A.P. Black. The A.P., by the way, stands for Andre Puyans, who created this series of nymphs. They are also commonly referred to as "all purpose" nymphs. These nymphs are universal in nature, and if a beginning flyfisher needed an assortment of nymphs, he couldn't go wrong with various A.P. Nymphs for an entire selection of nymphs. By adjusting colors and sizes, any flyfisher could be quite successful fishing this series of flies anywhere—including Alaska.

The dark moose hair and dyed black beaver-dubbed A.P. Black, though, is the all-star of the series for me. I tie it as large as size 8 and as small as size 18. As a testament to its effectiveness, I have to resupply my stock boxes with them after every season regardless of how many I have had time to tie during the previous winter.

My favorite way to fish the A.P. Black is on a floating line with a leader of about nine feet in length. I drift it through likely looking areas and concentrate on the tip of the fly line or part of the floating leader and look for the slightest hesitation, which signals a take. Cutts, dollies, and rainbows all find it attractive, and for grayling it's absolutely fatal. Especially when putting words into print, you learn to shy away from the words "always" and "never", but if there was ever a time to use them it would be where Black A.P. Nymphs and grayling are concerned. It wouldn't be too far from the truth to say that grayling are always receptive to and never refuse a well-presented A.P. Black.

Tying the A.P. Black

HOOK:	1x long nymph, e.g., Tiemco #3761, sizes 8-18
WEIGHT:	.025" lead
THREAD:	Black
TAIL:	Dark moose hair fibers
WING CASE:	Dark moose hair fibers
LEGS:	Dark moose hair fibers
RIBBING:	Copper wire
ABDOMEN:	Dyed black beaver underbody fur
THORAX:	Dyed black beaver underbody fur

1. Add weight to the front third of the hook shank. Secure, leaving the thread at the tail position.
2. Attach a tail of moose hair fibers. Work the thread forward to the back of the lead and tie in the fibers for the wing case. Return the thread to the tail position and tie in the copper wire.

3. Dub in the abdomen of the nymph up to the point where the lead begins. Rib the abdomen with the wire and tie off.
4. Dub fur over the lead for the thorax.
5. Fold the moose fibers forward over the thorax to make a wing-case and secure with the thread.
6. Force three fibers on each side of the hook toward the rear and hold in place with thread. These will be the legs.
7. Cut the remaining fibers as close as possible, cover with thread, and whip finish.

Flash Body Nymph

Unlike other nymph patterns, I don't tie on the Flash Body Nymph in the hopes of giving the fish the impression that this is a juicy, creepy-crawly main dish. Instead, it is meant to be more like a piece of candy. I think of it like the dish of jelly beans placed in front of guests. If they are like most people, no matter how emphatically they say, "No, thank you," they'll eventually succumb and begin eating them. This happens even after they have been served dinner. The Flash Body Nymph works on the same principle.

I've seen char, grayling, and trout that look like they're about to explode because of the number of eggs they've eaten. They become so full at times that even a well presented egg fly draws no response. The fish seem to be in a state of torpor, and repeated presentations with a variety of egg flies often will not even bring a close look and refusal, let alone a strike. In some cases, I have witnessed char so stuffed with eggs and listless that they actually lay motionless on the bottom of the stream. For a change of pace, and usually a strike, I switch to the Flash Body Nymph.

I doubt this silver-haloed, red-abdomened pattern actually represents anything that fish are accustomed to seeing, but it's exotic enough and has just the right touch of reality to gain the interest of overfed fish. It's somewhere between an impressionistic nymph and an attractor pattern. This trait undoubtedly accounts for its versatility and ability to take a variety of fish throughout the season in many different water conditions.

I originally tied this nymph with single strands of pearlescent Flashabou, but I have since found spooled pearlescent material of a wider diameter that makes covering the abdomen much easier. On occasion I'll use Flash Body Nymphs tied with floss and tying thread other than red. These substitutes, tied in colors such as green, black, and yellow, have turned some nice fish for me. However, the red version is far and away my favorite.

Tying the Flash Body Nymph

HOOK:	3x long nymph, e.g., Tiemco # 200, sizes 8 -14
WEIGHT:	.020" lead
THREAD:	Bright red
TAIL:	Black hackle fibers
BODY:	Pearl mylar wrapped over red floss
THORAX:	Peacock herl
HACKLE:	Black
WING CASE:	Mottled turkey quill

1. Weight the forward third of the shank with lead and secure, leaving the thread at the tail position.
2. Tie in the hackle-fiber tail and work the thread up to the back of the lead.
3. Tie in the quill for the wing case and return the thread to the tail position.

4. Tie in the floss and the mylar strip. Take the thread forward to the back of the lead.
5. Cover the abdomen with the floss and tie off.
6. Wrap the mylar over the floss abdomen and tie off.
7. Attach three strands of peacock herl and the hackle. Take the thread forward. Wrap the herl to form a thorax and tie off. Wrap the hackle forward and tie off.
8. Fold the quill forward and secure with thread to form the wing case. Whip finish.

Bitch Creek

There are no graceful lines or married feather wings to impress you here. This pattern is as rugged and as straightforward as its name—Bitch Creek. Obviously this fly isn't winning any points for its good looks or its mellifluous-sounding name. Then again it doesn't have to, because its reputation is solidly entrenched in Alaska—and throughout the western United States. After all, it consistently winds up lodged in the mouths of fish. In Alaska, it's a favorite of rainbows and many other fish. Cutthroats will get in line for it, grayling rarely refuse it, char find it irresistible, and when dragging it over the rocky shoals of lakes, lake trout will hit it with rod-jolting abandon.

In lakes or very slow moving waters I like to literally crawl a Bitch Creek across the bottom. I do lose a good share of flies to the bottom, but the number and often the large size of the fish I catch more than makes up for the number of flies I lose. I frequently keep a photograph on my tying table of a large fish with a Bitch Creek in its mouth. Glancing at the picture in the middle of the winter, I have no problem forcing myself to sit down and complete the couple of dozen Bitch Creeks that I know I'll need for the upcoming season.

Controlling the drift.

Fishing the Bitch Creek in running water is a simple matter of getting a good dead drift, as it is for most other nymph patterns. I think it's worth mentioning here that although I speak frequently of a dead-drift presentation, it's not quite that simple. A dead-drift presentation with any subsurface pattern is only effective if you remain in control. Anyone can accomplish dead drifts, but the fly may be at the end of so much slack line that they'll never realize when a fish strikes. Many times, because of the sheer number of what many anglers refer to as unsophisticated fish in Alaska, an angler mindlessly chucking a nymph into the water will wind up with a fish or two. It is the flyfisher who can fish a nymph—or an egg pattern for that matter—dead drift with control who will be far more successful.

This book is not a treatise on how to fish, so let me just say that there are lots of technical books and videos on the subject. If you're not familiar with things such as line mending, slack line, and reach casts, you need to do a little research on your own. Re-

member, though, that all the printed and film instruction in the world can't substitute for standing in the water and developing a feel for exactly what that unseen fly at the end of your line is doing. And if you happen to find yourself practicing some of these techniques in Alaska, there's probably no better fly to have at the end of your line than a Bitch Creek.

The Bitch Creek that I use has a woven abdomen. That is to say, I use what is commonly referred to as the half-hitch weave with two colors of chenille to form the two-toned abdomen of the fly. Some of the Bitch Creeks I have seen use the more simple method of tying a single strip of contrasting chenille over the top of the body, but I prefer the woven ones for the look they achieve and their increased durability. If you're not familiar with the half-hitch weave, you'll find valuable explanations and illustrations in Randall Kaufmann's *The Fly Tyer's Nymph Manual* (p. 148) and Eric Leiser's *The Book of Fly Patterns* (pp. 160-161).

I have found the Bitch Creek in more than a half dozen references on fly patterns, and all of the examples are slightly different in either tying method or color. The yellow-and-black color combination seems to be the most widespread, but in Alaska orange-and-black is my favorite. Second place, although it's a distant second, is occupied by the black-and-chartreuse combination.

Tying the Bitch Creek

HOOK:	3x long streamer, e.g., Mustad #9672, sizes 2-10
WEIGHT:	.030″ lead
THREAD:	Black
TAIL:	Two white rubber strips
ABDOMEN:	Black and orange chenille, black on top and orange below
THORAX:	Black chenille with brown palmered hackle
ANTENNAE:	Two white rubber strips

1. Weight only the portion of the hook shank that will become the thorax. Secure, leaving the thread in front of the lead.
2. Attach a pair of rubber strips in the front for antennae and at the rear for tails.
3. Attach sections of orange chenille and black chenille at the tail position. Wind the thread forward to the back of the lead. Using the half-hitch weave, work the two strands of chenille forward to the thread and secure. Cut the orange chenille but leave the remaining section of black chenille. (Alternatively, wrap the orange chenille to form the body. Tie off. Then bring the black chenille over the top to form the contrasting colors. Secure the black chenille but do not cut.)
4. Tie in the hackle. Wind the thread forward to the head.
5. Take the black chenille over the thorax and tie off. Palmer the hackle over the same area. Tie off and whip finish.

Brassie Nymph

This fly is the antithesis of an Atlantic salmon fly that incorporates dozens of materials in its construction. Forget about spending inordinate amounts of money on bits and pieces of strange animals from foreign lands. A hardware store will be your best source for the major component of this nymph—copper wire. Combine that with a hook, some thread, and a scrap of muskrat fur and you've got all the ingredients needed to create a deadly nymph.

You'll notice that I refer to this fly as a Brassie Nymph as opposed to just a Brassie. There is a distinction to be made, because, although they are similar, they're not the same fly. The Brassie has a copper wire body but also sports a white calf tail wing, where the Brassie Nymph has no wing at all. The Brassie is an effective sockeye salmon pattern while the Brassie Nymph, although it has resulted in some catches of sockeye salmon, is mainly used for trout, char, and grayling.

So what makes this nymph so deadly? Your guess, even if you haven't fished with this pattern or fished in Alaska, is as good as mine. Someone once gave me some rigamarole about it imitating certain species of caddisflies that select only yellowish and copper-colored minerals to make up their cases. Although I can't think of a plausible theory why a caddisfly would do that, it sounds feasible. After all, there are caddisflies that collect grains of sand and build spiral cases that resemble snail shells, so maybe there are species that have a penchant for metallic granules. I suppose I could pore over the pages in the volume by Wiggins or other notable works on Trichoptera, but some mysteries are better left alone so that they can remain, well, mysterious. Even if it is true, the problem is that I have yet to see any of these metal-loving caddis larva in Alaska, and using my trusty kick-net, I have looked at a whole lot of caddisflies in Alaska.

I keep looking, though, because there's this acquaintance of mine who is always picking up rocks along the stream. Instead of looking for insects, he's looking for gold. He even carries a gold pan with him sometimes when he's fishing. (Yes, they still pan for gold up here just like in the movies.) His plan is to locate a population of these caddis and move the larvae into a stream where he has found some color in his pan. The idea then would be to let these caddis larva spend the winter growing and making cases of small, metallic, yellowish grains of material, which in this stream would just happen to be gold. Then we would come back in the spring—before they emerge—and harvest these gold-cased caddis with kick nets. It's a ridiculously simple plan, and it would save your lower back from the drudgery of bending over a gold pan all day. I'm not putting much hope, or effort, into finding either the caddis or the gold, but if I just happen to have a set of Bogdan reels displayed next to my tackle closet next time you see me...

In the meantime I will continue to fish with the Brassie Nymph. Its only drawback is that it usually strikes out in slow water. Obviously it has nothing like the Wooly Bugger's marabou and hackle that will move or pulsate in slow currents. Because it's so heavy-bodied and sparse, it sinks like a little hunk of metal—which is essentially what it is—so it winds up on the bottom as opposed to drifting by a fish. Keep it in your box when you're on placid stretches of the stream, but definitely give it a try when riffles or pocket water have enough velocity to sport little patches of whitewater. The faster the water the better.

Rainbows, char, and grayling will gobble up a Brassie Nymph with equal zeal, and it is particularly effective for whitefish. Now before you sneer and say, "Who would want to catch a whitefish?" let me fill you in on a few things. There are several species of whitefish and ciscoes in Alaska, but one, the humpbacked whitefish, weighs three to five pounds, and occasional specimens will go to seven pounds. They run and jump when hooked, and it's not easy to entice them into taking a fly.

If I painted trout-like spots on their sides and changed their name, they would undoubtedly find their way on to the covers of many fine fishing publications. Let me put it this way, if you accidentally caught a four-pounder while you were trout fishing, you would probably try to recreate that accident on your ensuing casts, even if your buddies were downstream yelling, "Oh, it's just a whitefish."

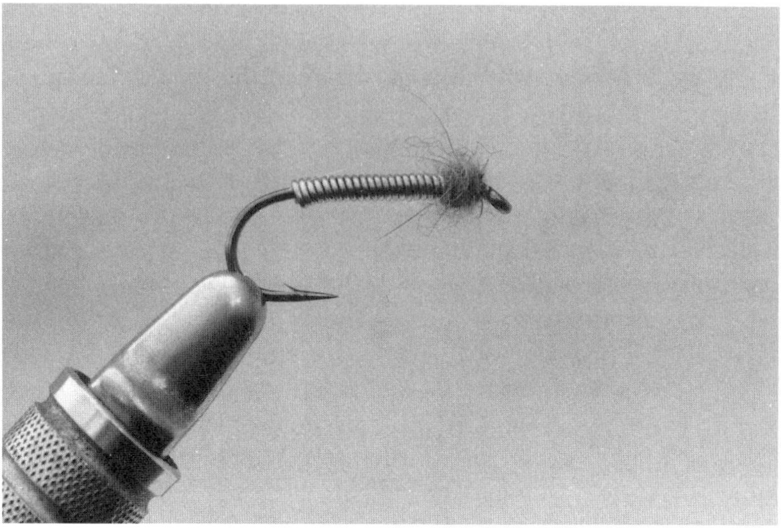

Tying the Brassie Nymph

HOOK:	2x strong nymph, Tiemco #3769, sizes 10-16
THREAD:	Black
BODY:	Copper wire
HEAD:	Muskrat underbody fur

1. Attach the thread two eye-widths behind the eye of the hook. Tie in a section of copper wire and, holding it parallel to and on top of the hook shank, cover it with the thread back to the tail position of the hook. Return the thread to the original tie-in position.
2. Wrap the wire forward to the thread and tie off.
3. Dub on a small portion of muskrat underbody fur. Whip finish.

Green Caddis Larva

There's a common misconception that Alaskan waters don't have much in the way of insect life. One fishing writer even wrote that "they are nearly devoid of aquatic insects." I guess those tumbling rivulets where surveys turn up substrate densities of blackfly larva in the hundreds per square foot or the streams where rocks are encrusted with hundreds of cased caddis don't count. Nor does it matter that the Katmai region even has a stonefly—*Isoperla katmaiensis*—named after it. I suspect that most reports on the lack of insects come from well-meaning people who, after spending a week here all caught up in egg feeding frenzies or flesh fly extravaganzas, simply forget to poke around in the substrate and take a good look for themselves. After all, when things are working well, why look beyond the obvious?

Like waters in more temperate areas of the world, Alaska's waters do have aquatic insects. The mayflies may be showier in other waters, and the stoneflies may be bigger. (*Isoperla katmaiensis*, for instance, is about three quarters of an inch long.) However, both insect groups, as well as caddisflies, are present.

Of all the caddisfly patterns that I have used in Alaska, the Green Caddis Larva has been the most consistent producer. That's not surprising when you consider the number of different caddis species found here that are green. There's the big free-living caddisfly of the genus *Rhyacophila* and lots of smaller species that make protective cases but are available to feeding fish. Because of the number of species found in Alaska, you can find specimens that range from bright green to olive drab. Regardless of what the locally predominant shade of green is, bright green always works best. If you are ever in doubt as to the correct color, err on the side of brightness. These fish obviously prefer something that resembles a mint julep rather than a martini olive.

I tie my Green Caddis Larva in both weighted and unweighted versions so that I can adapt my fishing technique to suit the water. Most of the time a dead drift is the simplest and most effective way to fish this fly, but quite often strikes will come after the drift when the fly is being lifted out of the water for the next cast. It is essentially the same rod-lifting technique often used to mimic the movements of an emerging pupa. Of course, this is a

Green Caddis Larva and is not supposed to imitate the emerging pupa, but rainbow trout, char, and especially grayling are attracted to it, so why argue with success?

Tying the Green Caddis Larva

HOOK:	3x long nymph, e.g., Tiemco #200, sizes 12-18
WEIGHT:	.020″ lead
THREAD:	Black
BODY:	Mint green dubbing, picked out
RIBBING:	Fine gold wire
HEAD:	Black dubbing

1. Wrap the lead over the front two-thirds of the hook shank. Secure, leaving the thread in the tail position.
2. Tie in a section of gold wire and then dub fur over the the hook shank leaving just enough room for a small bit of dubbing for the head.
3. Spiral the wire forward and tie off. Pick out the body dubbing.
4. Dub in a small portion of fur for the head. Whip finish.

Landing an Alaskan pink salmon.

Chapter 3: Subsurface Uglies
Fly and Season

	JAN	FEB	MAR	APR	MAY	JUN	JUL	AUG	SEP	OCT	NOV	DEC
Egg Sucking Leech				XX	XXX	XXX	XXX	XXX	XXX	XXX	X	
Wooly Bugger, purple				XX	XXX	XXX	XXX	XXX	XXX	XXX	X	
Wooly Bugger, chart./black				XX	XXX	XXX	XXX	XXX	XXX	XXX	X	
Marabou Girdle Bug					X	XXX	XXX	XXX	XXX	XXX	X	
A.P. Black					X	XXX	XXX	XXX	XXX	XX		
Flash Body Nymph					X	XXX	XXX	XXX	XXX	XX		
Bitch Creek					X	XXX	XXX	XXX	XXX	XXX	X	
Brassie Nymph					X	XXX	XXX	XXX	XXX			
Green Caddis Larva					X	XXX	XXX	XXX	XXX			

Chapter 3: Subsurface Uglies
Fly and Species

	KS	RS	CS	PS	SS	RT	ST	CT	CH	LT	AG	NP	SF
Egg Sucking Leech	X		X	X	X	X	X	X	X	X	X		
Wooly Bugger, purple	X				X	X	X	X	X	X	X		
Wooly Bugger, chart./black	X		X		X	X	X		X		X		
Marabou Girdle Bug					X	X	X		X		X		
A.P. Black						X		X	X		X		
Flash Body Nymph						X		X	X		X		
Bitch Creek						X	X	X	X	X	X		
Brassie Nymph		X				X		X	X		X		
Green Caddis Larva						X		X	X		X		

KS = King Salmon, RS = Red or Sockeye Salmon, CS = Chum Salmon, PS = Pink Salmon, SS = Silver or Coho Salmon, RT = Rainbow Trout, ST = Steelhead, CT = Cutthroat Trout, CH = Arctic Char/Dolly Varden, LT = Lake Trout, AG = Arctic Grayling, NP - Northern Pike, SF = Sheefish

Marabou Black Ghost, Thunder Creek, Woolhead Sculpin, Sea-Ducer, Lefty's Deceiver, Mickey Finn, Arctic Minnow, Olive Zonker

Chapter 4
A Streamer Selection

If you're an angler who likes to go after big fish, you know that streamers have a great track record. Strangely enough, a fairly high percentage of Alaskan anglers do not use streamer flies regularly. Here I must add a qualifier because many of those anglers would argue that their Bunny Flies, Alevins, Smolts, and Wooly Buggers are streamers and that they use them quite a bit. True enough. However, what I have in mind when I speak of a streamer is something more along the lines of a Mickey Finn, a Black-Nosed Dace, or a Gray Ghost, and it is these types of patterns that I see in very few numbers or altogether missing in many fly assortments.

Why this is, I'm not sure, and I will not speculate further. I will say, however, that I fish with streamers in Alaska quite frequently and have tremendous success when using them. This is the way I look at the situation. When I'm using a big streamer, I rarely hook

Sheefish and Deceiver.

into a 10-inch grayling. Instead I have a good chance of hooking into something that is capable of eating that 10-inch grayling. Need I say more?

Undoubtedly you will recognize some of these patterns, because in many areas of the country they are quite common. Why then, you might ask, do I include them here? First, they are excellent flies to use in Alaska, and second, they are flies you might not think to take on a fishing trip to Alaska. For instance, you are probably familiar with a Lefty's Deceiver, but have you thought about using it in Alaska? I'd be willing to bet that many anglers, whether they live in Alaska or outside the state, have an assortment of Lefty's Deceivers that are reserved exclusively for saltwater use. This is a mistake. Deceivers, as well as the other streamer patterns mentioned here, are great at drawing strikes from big Alaskan fish, but you have to use them to find out for yourself.

If you already have some of these flies, you can concentrate your efforts at the tying vise or money spent in a fly shop on some of the more unusual patterns found throughout these pages. In any case, don't forget to bring a selection of streamers with you to Alaska.

Marabou Black Ghost

I like tying flies with the new materials that seem to appear constantly, and I enjoy experimenting with many of the new fly patterns that come about as new applications are found for materials both new and old. However, I also have a fondness for many patterns that have been around for a long time. This fondness may in part be due to sentimentality, but it has more to do with the fact that some of those old flies catch a lot of fish. In fact, one of the traditional (some of my friends say that traditional is just a fancy term for old) streamers that I regularly use, because its success rate eclipses almost all others, is the Black Ghost.

The only thing that I have changed from the original dressing, as many others have, is the use of a white marabou wing instead of white saddle hackle. The marabou wing will, on occasion, get wrapped around the hook shank, but the fly's effectiveness far outweighs this disadvantage. For my personal tying, I retain the jungle cock eye called for in the original dressing just because I like the looks of it. It is one of the few flies for which I use my ever-dwindling supply of jungle cock. In the past I have replaced the jungle cock with a section of a wood duck barred flank feather or a yellowish-tipped body feather from a starling, and although the fly looks a little different in the vise, the fish don't seem to mind. But until my supply of jungle cock runs out, I will continue to splurge and use the real thing on this fly.

I use the Marabou Black Ghost throughout the fishing season, and it is often the first fly I tie on when nothing like an insect emergence or ravenous egg-feeding is taking place. I fish it an equal amount of time in lakes and streams, and it has accounted for a wide range of species from pike to cutthroat trout. In lakes I like to use it during the dim light of dusk (which occurs here anytime from early evening to late at night, depending on the time of year).

I fish the Marabou Black Ghost unweighted and use a variety of stripping sequences for the retrieve. Its main use for me is as a shallow-running fly, and consequently I usually fish it with a floating line in both lake and stream. When fishing it in moving water, I like to keep it very active. This means I usually cast straight downstream and use a strip retrieve or cast across-and-down while adding a strip or two during every two or three feet of drift.

Tying the Marabou Black Ghost

HOOK:	6x long streamer, e.g., Tiemco #300, sizes 2-8
THREAD:	Black
TAIL:	Yellow hackle fibers
BODY:	Black floss
RIBBING:	Flat silver tinsel
THROAT:	Yellow hackle fibers
CHEEK:	Jungle cock or substitute
WING:	White marabou

1. Attach a hackle fiber tail of approximately the same length as the gap of the hook.
2. Attach the tinsel and floss. Take the thread forward to just behind the eye of the hook. Wrap the floss forward to create a slim body and tie off. Spiral the tinsel over the body and tie off.
3. Attach hackle fibers the same length as the tail in the throat position.
4. Attach a jungle cock feather or substitute (see text) for the cheek.
5. In the wing position, tie in the marabou fibers so that they extend as far back as the end of the tail. Tie off and whip finish.

Thunder Creek

Ever since my first look at Keith Fulsher's book, *Tying and Fishing the Thunder Creek Series*, I knew I had to have some Thunder Creeks in my streamer box. They impressed me as being more fish-like than most of the other streamers that I'd been using. I tied several of the different patterns found in that book and fished with them for years, and they always performed well enough, at one time or another, to maintain them among my current selection of streamers. There was a time, though, when my carrying capacity and use of Thunder Creeks dropped off, owing either to a decrease in their effectiveness, a cadre of new streamer flies that I had to test, or sheer indifference, I'm not sure.

Then I became aware of some Thunder Creeks tied by an angling friend, Dirk Derksen, that got me all excited about Thunder Creeks again. The reports of the fish that he had caught with them had something to do with it, but what really intrigued me was the way they were tied. I don't think I am exaggerating too much when I say that a quick glance at a pile of these flies in a plastic box could be mistaken for nothing but unadorned long-shanked hooks. Sparse is a word we commonly use in conjunction with fly tying, but there should be a more definitive word to describe these flies. I was impressed by a fly that had almost no dressing and could be easily overlooked, yet managed to create the impression of a small fish. I tied some, fished them for a season, and was even more impressed by the way they worked. I now rely upon them heavily during times of low water.

When does low water occur? Good question. Often during the early part of the season—mid-May into June—water conditions are low because a large part of the water is still in the form of snowpack in the mountains and the glaciers haven't yet increased their output due to warming. Of course there are the years where unseasonably warm temperatures, combined with rain, can cause an early run-off and just as many years when it happens later than it should. By mid-July, water levels should decline until the rains of September, that is unless the rains come in late July or August. So, I guess the best answer to the question is, in Alaska low water occurs when the water is low. And when it does, don't be there without this sparse Thunder Creek streamer.

This pattern is not species specific. Lots of fish—rainbow trout, char, and grayling—like this pattern. I have to mention also that it's a very good fly to use when fishing for cutthroat trout in estuaries. The dressing below has changed a little from the ones that I previously described in other publications—it has gotten even sparser. Originally the pattern was tied with a silver tinsel body on a bronze hook, but when Tiemco came out with a 4x long, 3x heavy, nickel-plated streamer hook (#9394), I switched to it and omitted the silver tinsel body.

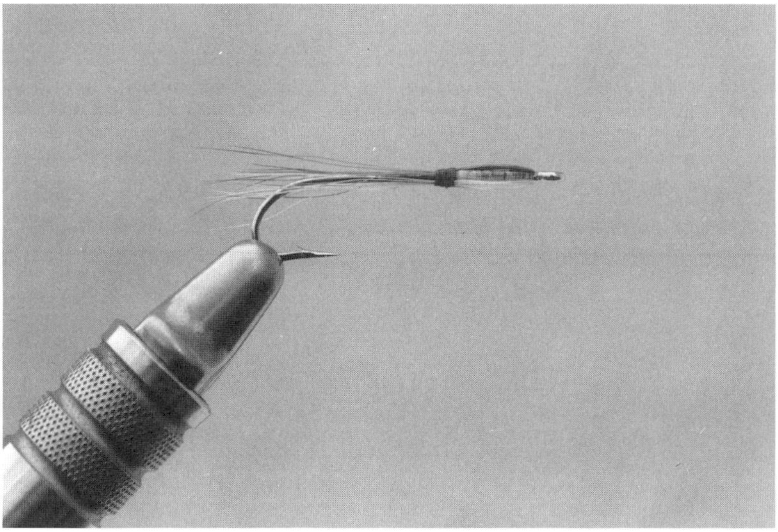

Tying the Thunder Creek

HOOK:	4x long, 3x heavy nickel-plated streamer, e.g., Tiemco #9394, sizes 8-10
THREAD:	White and red
BODY:	Top half brown bucktail, bottom half white bucktail

1. Attach the white thread one third of the hook shank's length behind the eye of the hook. Tie in the brown bucktail on top of the shank and the white bucktail underneath the shank, both projecting forward a shank length beyond the eye of the hook.
2. Work the thread forward so that it covers the bucktail from the

tie-in point to the eye of the hook and then return the thread to the tie-in point. Whip finish and cut the thread.

3. At this same point, attach the red thread to the hook shank. Now fold back the brown bucktail and make three wraps with the red thread to hold it there. Repeat the procedure with the white bucktail. Whip finish.

Rocky shoreline—sculpin territory.

Woolhead Sculpin

I don't believe there is a better all-around, all-season fly pattern for catching rainbow trout in Alaska than a Woolhead Sculpin. It can be used nearly everywhere. It has yielded trophy-size trout from unsuspecting chalk-blue glacial waters and likewise from the rocky shorelines of lakes. And it knows no seasonality. It has caught the attention of rainbow trout holding behind spawning salmon in July when logic would suggest that an egg pattern should be used. It consistently lures the huge rainbow trout of late September and October into striking, and it has even accounted for a few catches when some mild weather happens to set in during February or March and relatively crazy people, myself for instance, go out armed with a fly rod in search of open water.

The reason for this can be summed up in one word—opportunity. Game fish all over the state of Alaska have the opportunity to feed on sculpins because they are found in nearly all waters. There are several species of sculpins found in Alaska but by far the most common is the slimy sculpin (*Cottus cognatus*). These creatures, which are usually two to three inches long, can be found in lakes and rivers. Unlike some other forms of fish food, sculpins don't exhibit seasonal ups and downs of abundance. What better fly pattern could you have than one that imitates something that fish eat, is found in almost every watery habitat in Alaska, and is present throughout the entire year?

Although there is some color variation among sculpins, I find the Black Woolhead Sculpin the most useful. Even when samples of the naturals would suggest that a lighter or more olive color be used, the black version usually outperforms them.

The key to fishing the Woolhead Sculpin is simple, fish it deep, preferably on the bottom where possible. Fish it dead-drift, with a slow retrieve, with a fast retrieve, it doesn't matter, just get it deep. Sure, you'll lose plenty of these flies to snags, but that's part of the game—big risk, big fish.

While I may have emphasized its attractiveness to rainbow trout, it knows no bounds and does not discriminate among species. Cutthroat and lake trout, grayling, char, and even pike regularly pick up the sculpin for a quick meal, and, it has also been taken by some awfully big king salmon occasionally.

Tying the Woolhead Sculpin

HOOK:	3x long streamer, e.g., Mustad #9672, sizes 2-6
WEIGHT:	.030″ lead
THREAD:	Black
TAIL:	Rabbit strip left uncut so that it can be tied along the back of the fly Matuka-style
RIBBING:	15-pound monofilament
BODY:	Black chenille
PECTORAL FINS:	Grouse body feathers
WING:	Black rabbit strip, Matuka-style
HEAD:	Black wool trimmed to shape

1. Wrap the rear two-thirds of the hook shank with lead.
2. At the tail position tie in a rabbit strip leaving a tail equal to the length of the shank. Do not trim the remaining portion. Now tie in a six-inch piece of 15-pound monofilament and the chenille. Take the thread forward to the front of the lead.
3. Cover the rear two-thirds of the hook shank (the weighted portion) with the chenille and tie off.
4. Holding the remaining rabbit strip over the chenille-covered portion of the hook, work the monofilament through the hair

fibers, securing the rabbit strip in the Matuka style. Secure both the monofilament and the rabbit strip where the chenille ends.

5. Secure a grouse body feather on each side of the hook shank so that they splay outward at almost a 90-degree angle from the shank.
6. Making sure that the front third section of the shank has been completely covered with a base of thread, begin adding small amounts of wool in a manner similar to that of adding deer hair for spinning. Pack each clump onto the shank as tightly as possible and secure each successive clump with two or three wraps of thread. Once the shank has been completely covered, whip finish and cut the thread.
7. Taking care not to cut the rabbit strip or the grouse feathers, trim the head as you would trim spun deer hair. Remember a sculpin's head is not round. They have broad, relatively flat heads, so trim the wool shorter underneath and on top of the hook shank.

Sea-Ducer

In many areas, northern pike have gotten a bad rap from flyfishers, and I'll have to admit I'm not real fond of sinking a big streamer to depths of 15 feet and trolling for pike. When pike are up in the shallows, however, I think they are a lot of fun to catch.

In the past, whenever I have encountered pike in this situation, I reached for a big, colorful streamer, cast, and then retrieved the fly in quick foot-long strips with the hope that a pike would rush the moving fly and engulf it before taking too long of a look at it. The problem is, it didn't always happen that way. Pike have a habit of quickly moving behind a passing fly and then following it all the way to your rod tip without striking. Here, frustration is defined as having the pike race away in fear after you reach the point where there's no line left to retrieve and you have to wiggle the rod around to get enough line out to begin false casting.

Most of the time the solution is rather simple. Execute a series of fast strips, let the fly settle for five to 10 seconds and then begin stripping again. The strike may come anytime after the fly has begun to sink or just as the retrieve is resumed. While the solution is simple, carrying it out isn't always practical. Slim-profile streamers, even if they are unweighted, tend to sink so rapidly that, in water three feet deep or less where pike are the most fun to catch, the streamer will hit bottom long before you're ready to begin your retrieve. If the bottom consists of mud or sand this is no problem, but when there are weeds or other debris the fly will become lodged or pick up a big hunk of debris. Neither does anything to pique the interest of a pike. The complete solution is to use a Sea-Ducer.

Because the front portion is heavily hackled, Sea-Ducers sink slowly. Slowly enough so that even in three feet of water you can pause for five seconds without hooking the bottom. Consequently, you can use the strip-strip-strip-pause technique in shallow water and catch a lot of pike. You can attempt to do the same thing with flies made from rabbit strips which are often used for pike, but they sink much faster than a Sea-Ducer. Also, the rabbit strip flies become very heavy when wet. Assuming you don't want to use a monster-sized rod for pike, the Sea-Ducer is much easier to cast with a lighter outfit.

Lots of colors have been used to interest pike and sometimes one particular color will result in a banner day, but more often than not, you can't go wrong with a red-and-yellow color combination.

I know that you may not go out with the intention of catching pike, but in Alaska they are often found in close association with some of the more glamorous species. For instance, some fine rainbow trout rivers have weedy, backwater sloughs that are full of pike. Carrying a few Sea-Ducers will not take up much room in your vest, and if you do, you'll be able to take advantage of some awfully fun and often overlooked fishing.

Tying the Sea-Ducer

HOOK:	Saltwater or salmon wet fly, e.g., Mustad #34007 or #3407, size 3/0
THREAD:	Red
WING:	Red and yellow saddle hackles tied in at the tail position
HACKLE:	Red and yellow saddle hackles alternated to fill up the rest of the hook shank

1. At the bend of the hook, attach a set of four saddle hackles (three yellow and one red, with the red being the outermost feather) on each side of the hook shank so that they splay outward. Tie off.
2. Attach a red saddle hackle. Take the thread forward, covering one-third of the remaining hook shank. Wind the hackle forward as you would when hackling a dry fly and tie off. Repeat the procedure with a yellow hackle and then another red hackle, filling up the rest of the hook shank. Whip finish.

Lefty's Deceiver

Sometimes things can be so obvious that they go unnoticed. As the adage goes, you wouldn't know it if it hit you on the head. And to let the truth be known, I had hit myself on the head (plus a couple of strikes to the earlobe and shoulder) more than once with a Deceiver. It didn't help, though; I still hadn't noticed the obvious.

I'd tied Deceivers for years, even while living in Alaska, but I'd never caught a fish with them here. I didn't even fish them in Alaska. Instead I traveled with them. It seemed that no matter where I was going, if it was a saltwater fishing destination, Deceivers were always the first fly on my list. They were proven patterns that usually managed to draw the interest of big fish.

One Alaskan spring day all this changed. I was using an oversized nymph to scrape the bottom of a big pool created by the juncture of two streams, and for what seemed like the hundredth time that day, a juvenile silver salmon latched onto my nymph. Some of these little nuisances were only about three inches long, and it was incredible to think that anything so small would select such a big target for a meal and somehow manage to get hooked. The one that I had on at the moment, however, looked as though it would prove to be the trophy of the day. I hadn't caught any of the trout or char that I was after, and this fish would stretch the tape to six inches.

It's not unusual among a group of juvenile salmon to find some larger individuals. Some spend an extra season or two in freshwater and others just grow faster. The latter group would probably be considered—at least by anglers—to be the best of the breed, the ones that we assume grow up and become tomorrow's exceptional fish.

Anyway, there I was with this best-of-show silver salmon impaled on my nymph, and I realized that this one wasn't going to live to fight another day. The hook had penetrated something very important, because the fish was sliding along with the current vibrating and twirling in what was obviously the dance of death. I felt badly, but before I could pull it in to take a closer look, something big slammed into the struggling smolt and ripped it off of my nymph. The view from where I was standing—and I have a vivid picture of this in my memory—is of a large, dark shape and little specks of light reflected from the scales that were knocked loose from the small fish. I'm still not sure of the fish's identity. It could have been a rainbow trout, a char, or possibly a lake trout.

Determined to catch this big fish, I searched through my fly boxes for a big streamer. The biggest that I came up with looked very small in comparison to that six-inch smolt. None of my efforts worked and at the next available opportunity, I went through all of my flies I had stockpiled at home. The only ones that approached the length of that small, now digested, fish were Lefty's Deceivers. I'd love to be able to tell you that I returned to the same spot and caught a huge rainbow (or whatever) on a Deceiver, but it didn't happen. I returned and got skunked.

This event broke the barrier, though, and now I carry Deceivers all the time. Sometimes it does seem a little silly to select a three- to six-inch Deceiver and prepare to cast it into a stream that measures only 60 feet in width. However, with the number of large fish that I've since caught on a Deceiver, I do it without hesitation. Believe me, three to six inches of streamer will look huge even when put next to your salmon patterns, but to a five-pound char or trout, or a 15-pound sheefish, it represents nothing more than a small fish dinner.

Deceivers can be fished using a wide range of techniques, depending upon water conditions, your attitude, and the mood of the fish. Some days a straight downstream cast with a teasingly slow retrieve is infallible. At other times it gets the most attention when it is retrieved with a fast-paced strip directly across the current. The Deceiver will work at any time of year, because there are almost always small fish available to predators. It doesn't have to be mistaken for a juvenile salmon either; it could just as well represent the immature stages of any other fish, such as a trout, char, grayling, or whitefish.

Of all the colors that I have tried, the dressing below is my favorite for Alaskan waters.

Tying the Lefty's Deceiver

HOOK:	Saltwater or salmon wet fly, e.g., Mustad #34007 or #3407, size 1/0
THREAD:	White
WING:	White saddle hackles with an olive-dyed grizzly saddle hackle tied in on each side, strands of pearl Krystal Flash below the hook shank and copper Krystal Flash above the hook shank with white bucktail above and below
TOPPING:	Four strands of peacock herl the length of the saddle hackles
THROAT:	Orange rabbit fur
SHOULDER:	Grizzly hen neck feather

1. At a point one-third of the shank length behind the eye of the hook, attach two white saddle hackles and one olive-dyed grizzly on each side, with the grizzly the outermost feather.
2. Attach clumps of bucktail above, below, and on the sides of the hook shank so that they all extend well past the bend of the hook. Mixed in with these, attach a few strands of copper Krystal Flash above the hook shank and pearl Krystal Flash below.

3. Attach the topping of peacock herl.
4. Attach a clump of rabbit hair in the throat position.
5. Attach a shoulder of grizzly hen neck on each side of the hook shank. Cover the trimmed butt sections of the remaining material while forming a head with the thread. Whip finish.

Mickey Finn

Every September a lot of flyfishers congregate on a little stream in the Iliamna area. The main attraction is rainbow trout—big rainbow trout. It is no secret either, and on any given day you will likely encounter several other anglers, most of whom have arrived via the collection of floatplanes from surrounding lodges.

Colorful sockeye salmon sometimes pack the stream from bank to bank, making it seem as though there would be no room for any rainbows, but the salmon, of course, are exactly why the rainbows are there.

Occasionally these flyfishers will use flesh flies, sculpins, or Wooly Buggers, but more often than not, a single egg fly, or some other up-to-the-minute, dynamite version of the single egg, is the standard fare. Upon seeing the stream, many anglers assume that the fishing will be relatively easy, because it's not so large that you have to be a great caster, the rainbow trout are often plainly visible, and, of course, they are obviously feeding on eggs.

Things aren't quite that simple though, and often first-time visitors become frustrated by their lack of success. These fish get hounded on a regular basis by lots of anglers. Your patterns and presentation can't be as shoddy as if you were fishing on a much more remote stream for a four-year-old rainbow trout that had never seen an artificial fly. It's not uncommon to see two or three anglers doing most of the catching, especially of the bigger fish, while the rest do a lot of casting.

One day a couple of years ago, I had enjoyed reasonably good success in the morning but about midday, for whatever half-crazed reason, I decided to tie on a Mickey Finn. Then I decided to clean my line. When I was done, rather than making the usual short cast across the stream, I cast as much line as I could, with the wind, figuring that I could reel in the line through the line cleaner one last time. A steady wind was blowing upstream. When it finally came down, that Mickey Finn was a long way upstream from me.

It only took me a second to realize that I wasn't taking up line as fast as the current was pushing it back down at me, so I began making long, sweeping strips and loosely coiling the line on the ground when I felt the fly sink into something. My first thought was that I had foul-hooked a salmon. Then a huge rainbow thrashed on the surface and with my Mickey Finn in its mouth, swam, not upstream, but downstream directly at me. As it swam past, I got a good enough look at it to get more than a little bit excited, first because of its size and second because I had coils of fly line all over the place. Miraculously, the fly line managed to slip through the guides without tangling, and as the fish swirled on top about 45 yards downstream from me, another angler walking up the bank let out a very loud expletive. A couple of other anglers noticed the excitement and were soon standing by my side as I moved downstream in an attempt to regain line.

After a few introductory comments came the inevitable question, "What fly are you using?"

As calmly as I could, I replied, "A Mickey Finn." All the Iliamna Pinkies stuck in the fly patch on my vest didn't help the situation any, and to say that they didn't believe me is grand understatement.

The angler who had been closest to me and had first seen the fish said something like, "You mean to tell me I've been trying to catch one of those big——rainbows all morning and you've been catching them on a——Mickey Finn. What a stupid fly."

Evidently he'd been keeping an eye on my earlier efforts, but I didn't have time to tell him that this was the first cast with a Mickey Finn before the fish showed itself a couple of more times and, as quickly as it had struck, was gone. And so was my proof that I had been using a Mickey Finn—it had broken off. Of the onlookers' various size estimates, none were close to 10 pounds. They were all much higher, and I'll leave it at that—it was a very big rainbow trout.

I will admit that a Mickey Finn was not the preferred fly to use in that situation nor was the technique of casting straight upstream and stripping in the line as fast as I could the preferred tactic, but it worked. Nor was this the first time that I had hooked a large fish on a Mickey Finn. I have used Mickey Finns as long as I have fished in Alaska, and they have always produced well for me. Typically, I like to cast them across the current and let them swing unimpeded and then retrieve them back upstream in short, quick strips. They perform equally well in lakes and streams. They have produced cutthroat and lake trout, steelhead, char, grayling, and pike, as well as rainbow trout.

Deviating from the original dressing, I omit the oval silver ribbing and use red instead of black thread. I also use a body of mylar tubing which makes it much easier to cover the lead when I'm tying weighted versions.

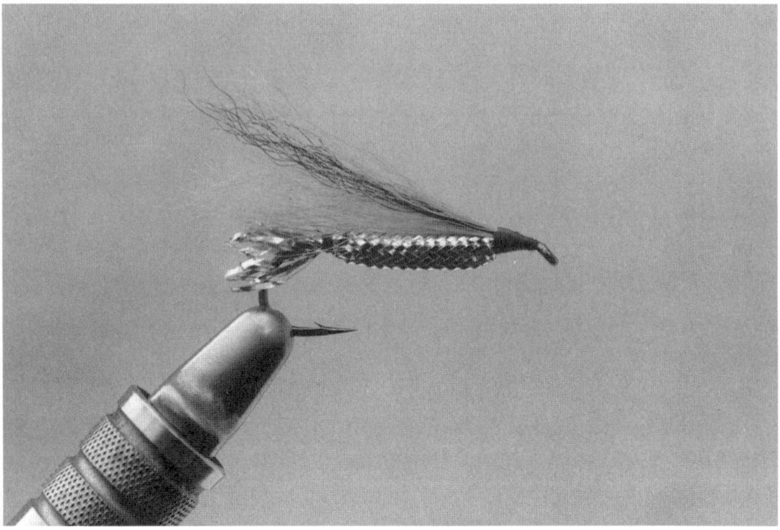

Tying the Mickey Finn

HOOK:	2x long streamer or nymph, e.g., Tiemco #5262, sizes 2-10
WEIGHT:	.035″ lead
THREAD:	Red
BODY:	Silver mylar tubing
WING:	Yellow over red over yellow bucktail or calf tail

1. Wrap the hook shank with lead from a spot directly above the point of the hook to a distance of two eye-widths behind the eye of the hook. Secure, leaving the thread at the tail position.
2. Slide a section of mylar tubing over the hook shank allowing the unraveled end to work through the thread and extend beyond the bend of the hook. Secure with thread, whip finish, and cut the thread.
3. Reattach the thread behind the eye of the hook and secure the front end of the mylar tubing.
4. Attach three layers of bucktail or calf tail in a yellow/red/yellow sequence. Whip finish.

Arctic Minnow

You can't help but be amazed when you watch an Arctic tern hover 20 feet above the water, partially close its wings, dive, and come up with a two-inch fish. Just spotting a subsurface fish from that distance, never mind diving and picking it off, is impressive. To me, the visual acuity necessary to perform this maneuver is unimaginable. Wherever Arctic terns are found in Alaska, it's not uncommon to have one dive at a shallow-running fly only to break the assault off in midflight when it decides the fly isn't real. On two occasions terns have dived, hit, and picked up my fly, and both times I was using a fly which I later named the Arctic Minnow. I am not espousing an open season on Arctic terns, but I do feel quite good that the fly is realistic enough to fool a sharp-eyed bird. Now you may be saying to yourself, big deal, will it fool fish? You bet! Fish hit it with a lot less hesitation than do Arctic terns.

I will admit to creating this pattern and its name, but in no way do I take credit for this type of fly. Fashioning a fish-imitating fly out of deer hair is nothing new, and although I haven't seen any others with a belly-strip of Flashabou there are probably some out there somewhere. My first attempts with a fly similar to this—the Charles E. Brooks' Floating Minnow—were met with success, but the fly, at least the way I tied it, didn't float well and had a tendency to self-destruct after not too much use. This may have been a design flaw in the original quill-bodied Floating Minnow, but could have been more a result of the way I put it together. I looked for another pattern that would fish the same way and didn't find any, so I set about making my own. Rather than take you through the several years' worth of prototypes, suffice it to say that the Arctic Minnow is the culmination of a long trial-and-error period.

Many species of Alaskan game fish find the Arctic Minnow irresistible, but rainbows, char, and pike are the most susceptible. Don't be surprised, though, when a large grayling comes up and smashes into it. They also take advantage of smaller, less fortunate, fish. Fish it across, up- or downstream, it doesn't matter. Just get yourself set up so that you can let it drift with the current and then twitch it repeatedly. In short, make a commotion on the water's surface with it. In reality, it doesn't float too well, and

once it is waterlogged it does little more than ride in the surface film rather than on it. This is exactly when it's at its deadliest.

I can't say that I've seen a small fish naturally doing whirligig motions near the surface of the water. I have witnessed a few small fish that were released by anglers who employed a vise-like death grip while they removed the hook. The fish then spun haphazardly around on top of the water while the current swept them downstream. Extrapolating from this, I can only figure that a fish injured due to a natural event would probably respond in the same fashion. Although it may not happen too often, when it does, predators react quickly.

I liken it to the way a shark or barracuda will appear out of nowhere and demolish a fish that you have been fighting for a while. The factors that account for this shark-feeding intensity are undoubtedly manyfold, but you can be sure of one thing—when it hits an Arctic Minnow, a fish will be neither slow nor indecisive. It will hit swiftly and it will hit hard. It's almost as if the attacker figures it has to get this dying fish before a neighbor does.

Tie some Arctic Minnows (because I doubt you'll be able to buy them anywhere) and try them whenever and wherever you are in Alaska, because a predator's response to an easy meal makes for unforgettable fishing.

Tying the Arctic Minnow

HOOK:	Wide gap (stinger), e.g., Mustad #37187, size 2
THREAD:	White
TAIL:	White rabbit strip and pearlescent Flashabou
BODY:	Trimmed antelope hair with remaining strips of Flashabou stretched along the underside and tied off at the head

1. Attach 12 strands of Flashabou in the tail position. The Flashabou should be two shank-lengths long and should be attached so that half the length extends back for the tail. The other half will later be stretched forward under the belly of the fly.
2. Attach a shank-length tail of rabbit strip over the Flashabou. Tie off.
3. Spin and tightly pack antelope hair all the way from the tail position to just behind the eye of the hook, leaving room for a small head. Trim into an elongated cigar shape.
4. Stretch the remaining Flashabou under the body from the tail to the thread. Secure it with several wraps of thread to form a small head and tie off. Whip finish.

Olive Zonker

There are many different species of forage fish in Alaska that flyfishers knowingly or unknowingly imitate. Some of the examples we have seen thus far are the Blue Smolt, which imitates juvenile salmon, the Woolhead Sculpin, which, of course, imitates a sculpin, and a Lefty's Deceiver, which may simply be attractive to fish but can be used to imitate many species of fish found in Alaska. Another fly that I have found very advantageous to have is an imitation of the ubiquitous stickleback.

There are actually two species, the Threespine and the Ninespine Stickleback, but for fly tying purposes, there isn't any reason to distinguish between the two. Though it does seem at times that they are almost everywhere, I haven't encountered sticklebacks in the interior portion of the state, and a quick check of Morrow's *The Freshwater Fishes of Alaska* shows that to be the case. Their range is limited to a band which shadows the coastline of Alaska, reaching well inland in many cases but not to the central interior portion of the state.

Their color varies from an olive brown to a greenish color, but I have not found it necessary to carry patterns to match the various color phases. Instead I carry just one pattern, the Olive Zonker. It's a good color compromise, and the fish will not snub it if the naturals where you're fishing happen to be a shade or two lighter or darker. For some time I alternated between the Olive Zonker and an Olive Matuka when imitating sticklebacks, but on almost every occasion the Zonker wound up being the fly of preference, and I no longer carry the Matukas. The difference, I think, is that bit of flash provided by the body of a Zonker which you don't find on a Matuka. Looking down on a real stickleback in the water, you may not realize why the shine is so important. If you get one to roll over or pick it out of the water, you'll see that their sides are quite silvery.

Sticklebacks coexist with trout, char, grayling, and pike in many rivers and lakes. Some studies have shown that juvenile rainbow trout have to compete with the sticklebacks for food. Once the rainbows grow to a certain size, the tables are turned, and they eat the sticklebacks. Usually sticklebacks are about two to three inches in length, and a Zonker that approximates that

Which streamer?

size is a good choice although fish will sometimes hit a much larger pattern.

An Olive Zonker, like many of the other baitfish patterns, can be used regardless of the season since baitfish are always in the water and available to predators. I use a fairly quick but erratic retrieve with the Zonker in both rivers and stillwater to mimic the frenetic movements which characterize the stickleback's behavior. The Olive Zonker has been responsible for some fine catches for me in the past years, including one lake trout that I would have had trouble hefting from the water up to the edge of my float tube for a photograph if someone had been there to take a picture.

Northern pike will often savagely attack Olive Zonkers, and rainbow trout and char take them with great energy, while the grayling do less so. Some sticklebacks venture into saltwater, and I have occasionally had great luck fishing the Olive Zonker in estuaries for sea run cutthroat and Dolly Varden. Where sticklebacks are found, there are so many of them available as prey that you shouldn't be without a good imitation, and that imitation is the Olive Zonker.

Tying the Olive Zonker

HOOK:	4x long streamer, e.g., Tiemco #9394, sizes 2-6
THREAD:	White
TAIL:	Olive rabbit strip
BODY:	Pearl mylar tubing with an underbody of metallic tape to fill out the belly
WING:	Olive rabbit strip from tail along the back to the eye of the hook
HACKLE:	Grizzly dyed olive tied in as a collar

1. Fold a piece of metallic tape over the hook shank. It should extend from directly above the barb of the hook to a point two eye-widths behind the eye of the hook. The metallic tape should extend no more than half of the gap width below the shank of the hook.
2. At a point one third of the shank length behind the eye make two angle cuts, one tapering forward to the eye of the hook and one tapering to the bend of the hook.
3. Slide a piece of mylar tubing over the hook shank and the trimmed metallic tape. Let the unraveled portion of the mylar extend just beyond the bend of the hook and secure the tubing

with several wraps of the thread. Whip finish. Cut the thread, leaving a six-inch portion to be used later.

4. Reattach the thread just behind the eye of the hook and secure the front portion of the mylar tubing.
5. Attach a rabbit strip approximately twice the length of the hook shank.
6. Attach and make a collar with two or three wraps of a hackle. Form a head and whip finish.
7. Stretch the rabbit strip along the top of the hook shank and with the thread left at the bend of the hook, secure the rabbit strip with several wraps, being careful to work it through the guard hairs of the rabbit as opposed to matting them down. Whip finish.

Chapter 4: A Streamer Selection
Fly and Season

	JAN	FEB	MAR	APR	MAY	JUN	JUL	AUG	SEP	OCT	NOV	DEC
Marabou Black Ghost					X	XXX	XXX	XXX	X			
Thunder Creek					XX	XX		X	XX			
Woolhead Sculpin			XX	XXX	XXX	XXX	XXX	XXX	XXX	XXX	XX	
Sea-Ducer					XXX	X		X	XX			
Lefty's Deceiver			XX	XXX	XXX	XXX	XXX	XXX	XXX	XXX	XX	
Mickey Finn					XX	XXX	XXX	XXX	XX			
Arctic Minnow						XXX	XXX	XXX	XX			
Olive Zonker					XX	XXX	XXX	XXX	XX			

Chapter 4: A Streamer Selection
Fly and Species

	KS	RS	CS	PS	SS	RT	ST	CT	CH	LT	AG	NP	SF
Marabou Black Ghost						X		X	X	X	X	X	
Thunder Creek						X		X	X		X		
Woolhead Sculpin						X		X	X	X	X	X	
Sea-Ducer												X	
Lefty's Deceiver	X				X	X			X	X		X	X
Mickey Finn						X	X	X	X	X	X	X	
Arctic Minnow						X			X	X	X	X	X
Olive Zonker						X		X	X	X	X	X	X

KS = King Salmon, RS = Red or Sockeye Salmon, CS = Chum Salmon, PS = Pink Salmon, SS = Silver or Coho Salmon, RT = Rainbow Trout, ST = Steelhead, CT = Cutthroat Trout, CH = Arctic Char/Dolly Varden, LT = Lake Trout, AG = Arctic Grayling, NP - Northern Pike, SF = Sheefish

Katmai Slider, Simple Shrew, Hornberg, Blue-Winged Olive, Green Bomber, Little Yellow Stonefly, Rio Grande Trude, Humpy

Chapter 5
Topwater Models

A tremendous amount of ink has been used to print descriptions of fishing in Alaska. If you amassed all this printed material, read everything—all the books, articles, and advertisements—and then carefully catalogued and indexed the whole collection of flies mentioned, you would find that the list for dry flies would be a short one. The reason for this is quite simple. Dry flies are not used very much in Alaska.

There are, however, anglers (including myself) who use dry flies in Alaskan waters regularly, and there are some enlightened lodge operators and guides who encourage their clients to use dry flies in many situations. In fact, there are some Alaskan flyfishers, and visiting anglers as well, who plan trips during June specifically to fish with dry flies. I do just that on a yearly basis and am rarely disappointed. But taking into account all of the flyfishing done in

Alaska, the occasions when dries are used and the length of time they are fished is infinitesimal.

With this information you may assume, as many people do, that dry flies are not effective in Alaska. While I'll be the first to admit that dry flies are not a big component in the overall scheme of flyfishing in Alaska, if you think that they don't work, you're dead wrong. There's a time and a place for everything, and there are times and places in Alaska when dry flies are incredibly effective. Rarely are the opportunities as obvious as they may be in other places where a mass emergence of insects and the resultant rising fish are a common occurrence. There are times in Alaska when aquatic insects emerge in concentrated numbers, and there are times when fish, during one of these emergences or at other times, can be seen rising. Using a dry fly in either of these situations will often be met with success. The problem is that most of the time there are no visible signs to tip off the angler that a dry will work.

A case in point is the Brooks River in southwestern Alaska. It's widely known for its rainbow trout fishing, and anglers frequently use dry flies there. Why? Simply because the water looks like such beautiful dry fly water that long ago someone tried a dry fly and it worked. Now anglers have no reservations about fishing dry flies for rainbow trout in the Brooks River even though it's uncommon to see rising fish. Furthermore, they'll even fish a dry, and are successful at it, when the river is full of spawning sockeyes and the rainbows should be feeding on nothing but eggs.

Dry flies will elicit strikes from Arctic grayling, most notably, but also from rainbow, cutthroat and lake trout, northern pike, char, steelhead, and silver salmon. More fish would be caught on the dry fly if more anglers used dry flies while fishing in Alaska. Understandably, in many situations (as is the case in other places) more fish can be caught by probing the depths rather than skittering flies across the surface, but please, don't become one of the anglers who perpetuate the myth that dry flies are of little or no use in Alaska.

I think you will find the following assortment eclectic, to say the least. In keeping with the book's theme, I have selected patterns that will work well and provide you with an assortment that will take you through an entire season. I would, however, like to make special mention of some flies I did not include. There are many well-known dry flies—the Adams, the Elk Hair Caddis, and the Wulffs, for instance—that will interest a variety of Alaskan fish. These flies are of such a universal nature and are so thoroughly described in other books that it is unnecessary to describe them here. Furthermore, anglers who fish with an Adams or an Elk Hair Caddis will undoubtedly include them in their travel kits anyway. An exception among the flies described in this chapter might be the Blue-Winged Olive. These diminutive flies could easily be left at home when anglers venture to Alaska. I chose to highlight it, because it's a good pattern to have in Alaska and because so few anglers associate it with Alaska that it could easily be overlooked.

Before moving on to the patterns, I want to draw your attention to a technique that can be used with all dry flies in Alaska. That is, twitching or adding movement to an otherwise dead-drifting fly. I realize that even the suggestion of intentionally interrupting a not easily achieved drag-free float provides more than enough ammunition for dry-fly fishers to label me a heretic. But it does work, and if you don't try it, you'll miss out on some fun fishing. Here's how it works.

When you've spotted a fish or likely looking holding water, make several typical dead drift presentations. If they fail to draw a strike, the logical step would be to try a different pattern. So far, so good, but when enough patterns fail that you begin to think that the fish simply will not come up for a dry, it's time to try a twitch. Set up for another dead drift but this time quickly pull the line, causing the fly to skip forward an inch or two when it's still a couple of feet in front of the fish. One of three things will happen: the fish will take the fly, the fish will race away in fear, or the fish will not move. If it takes the fly, great. If it bolts, well, at least you tried several dead drifts the way it's supposed to be done first. If the fish doesn't move, try the twitch again, and with each successive try, increase the commotion level. This can be done by stronger pulls on the line and by increasing the size of the fly. There are times when I have followed this strategy all the way up to where I was chugging a size 2 Bomber through the water like I was bass fishing with a Hula Popper. More often than not, somewhere long before this stage, the fish will hit the fly.

A Katmai Slider against the bank.

At this point you might be thinking, and rightfully so, that this seems like an awful lot of work for just one fish in a land where the fishing and the catching is reputed to be easy. It is a lot of work, and I will not deny that the fish in question might not hesitate if presented with an outsize Wooly Bugger or Woolhead Sculpin. There comes a time, however, when you're staring at a slowly finning rainbow trout that is slightly larger than the biggest salmon you caught on the previous day and you want to see for yourself exactly what kind of surface swirl a fish like that makes coming up for a dry. When you've reached this point, start twitching and hang on.

Now having fully ensconced myself as a heretic where dry-fly maneuvers are concerned, I will mention one more facet of dry-fly fishing in Alaska that will easily propel me well beyond the group that memorizes emergence tables and practices the correct pronunciation of Latin names. If it wasn't for the fact that I have only used them thoroughly for just over one season (and consequently they haven't met the proven-over-time requirement for the flies described here), I might be including poppers in this collection of dry flies. That's right, poppers, those brightly colored cork-bodied things typically reserved for farm ponds and panfish.

On a number of outings last season the rainbow trout just loved poppers, especially the kind made with foam instead of cork. Big rainbows, too. Some of them threw caution to the wind and hit those big soft-bodied poppers that look much more at home on some mangrove-filled snook water in Florida. Only time will tell, but I will definitely be trying out more of them in the future. You might, if it doesn't offend your sense of dry-fly purism, take some along if you're destined for Alaskan rainbow trout water.

Katmai Slider

This is my favorite fly when it comes to dry-fly fishing in Alaska. Why? In terms of versatility, it is matched only by the Hornberg, and most importantly, I catch a lot of fish while using it. It is the result of a lengthy evolutionary process that began with a mouse pattern, and although it more closely resembles a steelhead Greased Liner, it was long before it gained its present form that it was christened the Katmai Slider.

Its need and its development began on a very windy day when the rainbow trout were in the mood to smash any mouse pattern that floated into view. To get the big, bulky, wind-resistant mouse pattern out where it had to be required a heavy rod and a mean disposition. Even then, the line would straighten out only until the mouse caught some wind and settled well downwind whether you were casting that way or not. The trout were not really big, but there were lots of them.

I really would have preferred to catch them with something like a four- or five-weight, but the combination of the wind, that big, air-resistant fly, and a lightweight rod was beyond my casting capabilities. So instead I tried, without too much success, the biggest Elk Hair Caddis I had in my box, a size 6. That day began the progression of prototypes which resulted in the Katmai Slider. In style, it is so similar to the Greased Liner that you might argue that I was reinventing the wheel, but at no time did I think of the Greased Liner until after the Slider's successful maiden voyage. Then someone looked at it and said, "Nice fly, looks like a Greased Liner." So it does, and it works.

I have tried them for several seasons now in countless colors, including variations of both the wing and body material, but none catch as many fish as the dressing prescribed below with natural deer hair and a white poly-yarn body. I still carry Katmai Sliders in other colors—fluorescent orange, yellow, and lime green—and they have turned the trick on an odd day or two when every other floating pattern, including the natural and white Katmai Slider, has failed to raise a fish.

While going through my notes I found that an orange-winged version seems to give better results during the twilight hours, which here in Alaska can mean as late as midnight or 1 a.m. if you happen to be fishing on a cloudless day during the months of June or July. Why the orange-winged version produces during twilight, I'm not sure, and I can't say that I even recognized the trend until I checked my notes. It could be that I just select the orange fly for better visibility once the light begins to fade. This would mean that it spends more time on the water during the low light hours and therefore takes more fish.

The Katmai Slider has gotten plenty of strikes from rainbow trout and grayling as it floats dead drift downstream, but the most effective way to fish it is to cast across and downstream and allow it to drag and create a wake over a fish or suspected holding spot. If you're going to be successful in taking a steelhead or a silver salmon on the surface in Alaska, this is the technique that will most likely do it for you. In fact, it was with a Katmai Slider that I enticed my first steelhead to a dry fly in Alaska. In three days of fishing nothing but surface patterns, I managed to hook and land three steelhead on this pattern last season. To date they are the only dry-fly caught steelhead that I have taken in Alaska. Late in the season, say around September, this waking presentation will also encourage char to come to the surface. These will not always be your run-of-the-mill char either. I've taken char in excess of eight pounds using this technique with a Katmai Slider.

Tying the Katmai Slider

HOOK:	1x long, 1x fine salmon dry fly, e.g., Mustad #9049, sizes 2-6
THREAD:	Bright orange
TAIL:	Natural deer hair
BODY:	White poly yarn
HACKLE:	Grizzly
WING:	Natural deer hair with butts exposed and trimmed

1. Attach a tail of deer hair that is approximately as long as the gap of the hook.
2. Attach a piece of white poly yarn and take the thread forward to a point two eye-widths behind the front of the hook. Wrap the yarn forward forming a smooth body. Tie off.
3. Attach a grizzly hackle feather and, after making two or three wraps, position the fibers so that they are swept back and underneath the shank of the hook. Secure with the tying thread.
4. Attach a clump of deer hair at the front of the hook as you would when tying an Elk Hair Caddis. The tips of the hair should not extend beyond the end of the tail. Pull down on the thread tightly so that the hair flairs. Trim the butt sections closely to form a head and whip finish.

Simple Shrew

You can't come to Alaska without a mouse pattern. Regardless of what time of year you're coming and exactly where you're going, you cannot take the chance of being somewhere where you might be able to use one and not have one. Taking a rainbow trout on a dry fly is one thing, but watching an oversized rainbow wallow around on the surface doing its imitation of a bass going for a duckling is something you just have to see. This is exciting stuff and shouldn't be attempted by those who are weak of heart!

Although this pattern is called the Simple Shrew, it is basically meant to imitate any small mammal that may, willingly or unwillingly, wind up swimming around in the vicinity of a rainbow trout. The flies that you will see offered for sale fall under a variety of names such as Mouserat, Alaska Lemming, or, simply, Mouse. While a quick check of an Alaska species list shows eight species of shrews, nine of voles, five of mice, and four of lemmings, I had often wondered why, sometimes in very unlikely circumstances, a rainbow would move up through several feet of water to hit one of these flies and whether something completely unlike a mouse, say a red-and-yellow Hula Popper, might entice them to do the same thing.

Two years ago, however, I got a partial answer to why rainbows come up for mouse patterns. I was floating a river in southwest Alaska during September and one evening I had drawn the duty of filtering the next day's drinking water supply. I sat on the end of the raft which projected out into the current and pumped water into our assortment of water bottles. While doing so, I watched a small mammal, which I supposed to be a red-backed vole, swim across the stream leaving a v-shaped wake in its path. It was late at night, almost dark, and before long I saw several others do the same thing.

I have no idea why so many of these voles decided it was time to cross the stream, but they kept it up at regular intervals. When the sixth or seventh took the plunge, something from below decided it was time to eat one. The vole disappeared in a splashy swirl of water. I was still marveling at what I saw when the same thing happened again farther upstream. You may guess what I did next, and yes, I did catch a football-shaped rainbow trout on a

mouse pattern. Since then, I haven't traveled anywhere in Alaska without mouse patterns somewhere among my fishing gear.

I have tried a variety of mouse patterns, including those that are detailed enough to include eyes, ears, nose, and tail. I think the Simple Shrew is as good as any of these patterns. The fish will hit the patterns that have all the details, but they are no less interested in the flies that don't have them, so I skip the intricacies of cutting out ears and burning monofilament for eyes.

If you read any of the fishing periodicals, you've probably read about fishing mouse patterns in Alaska, and most of the articles recommend fishing them close to undercut banks or casting very close to bank-side vegetation. I will not deny that these strategies work, but you should not overlook midstream currents even if the water is quite deep. I have caught just as many fish from these midstream areas as I have near the bank, sometimes in surprisingly deep water and where currents are so strong that they swamp the fly as it tails out on its swing.

The Simple Shrew is also an excellent fly to use for pike when they're in shallow, weedy bays or coves. Pike find the pattern irresistible when it's cast close to weeds or other obstructions and then slowly teased into deeper water.

Tying the Simple Shrew

HOOK:	Wide gap (stinger), e.g., Mustad #37187, size 2
THREAD:	Black
TAIL:	Natural brown rabbit strip
BODY:	Spun deer or antelope hair trimmed to shape

1. At the tail position, tie in a shank-length piece of rabbit strip.
2. Spin deer or antelope hair from this point forward to the eye of the hook. Whip finish and trim to shape, taking care to trim the bottom close to the shank so that the body will not interfere with hooking capability.

Hornberg

The Hornberg was one of the first dry flies I tried, and today it still maintains a fairly good reputation in the New England area where I used it. While spending a few years in the Great Lakes region where the Hornberg was created, I was surprised to find that few anglers I encountered used or even knew of the Hornberg. For the years that I was there, I used it with good results just as I had done while fishing it in the New England states. Once in Alaska I assumed that I wouldn't see much of the Hornberg, and as of this writing I have not seen any other flyfishers in Alaska using a Hornberg or even carrying one in their fly boxes.

I'm not sure why it hasn't gained popularity in Alaska, because for me it is often one of the first dry flies that I knot to my tippet. It's not my single best dry fly, but in terms of versatility it's very close to being number one. What other fly can you drift downstream like a dry fly and then strip back upstream underwater like a streamer? It's no mistake either, the Hornberg was designed for the purpose of being fished both as a dry and as a streamer fly.

One August while fishing a stream in the Bristol Bay region, I watched as a grayling came completely out of the water, as they will sometimes do, and try to hit my dead-drifting Hornberg on the way back down into the water. I failed to hook that grayling, but as the Hornberg, now submerged, continued on downstream I got another strike and this time a solid hook-up. The second fish turned out to be a rainbow trout, and immediately after I released it I made a notation in my notebook. Not because of the rainbow's strength or size but because of the unusual sequence of events. As far as I can remember, it was the only time I missed a grayling taking a dry fly and then hooked a rainbow trout on a streamer all on one cast with one fly. Whenever someone points to a Hornberg in my fly box and asks what it is, I always tell that story to illustrate its effectiveness and versatility.

I fish the Hornberg in sizes 6 through 16. I usually reach for it when conditions, such as high water, wind, and rain, aren't particularly conducive to fishing a dry fly, but I still want to give one a try. During these times it has the advantage of picking up fish while it is being fished as a streamer if nothing decides to rise for it. Its biggest advantage to me, however, has been one of a learning process. Since I regularly use it during times when you wouldn't normally expect a dry fly to work, I have been quite surprised and enjoyed some great dry-fly fishing when I wouldn't have otherwise even tried one. It has probably been the most important fly in shaping my opinion that the biggest reason more fish aren't caught on dry flies in Alaska is because dry flies aren't used all that much.

Obviously, when fishing it as a dry fly, it should be dead drifted, but don't forget to give it a twitch or two when fish seem unwilling to surface. When fishing it as a streamer, you can let the belly of the line swing it across current or retrieve it in a series of strips. Either method will work.

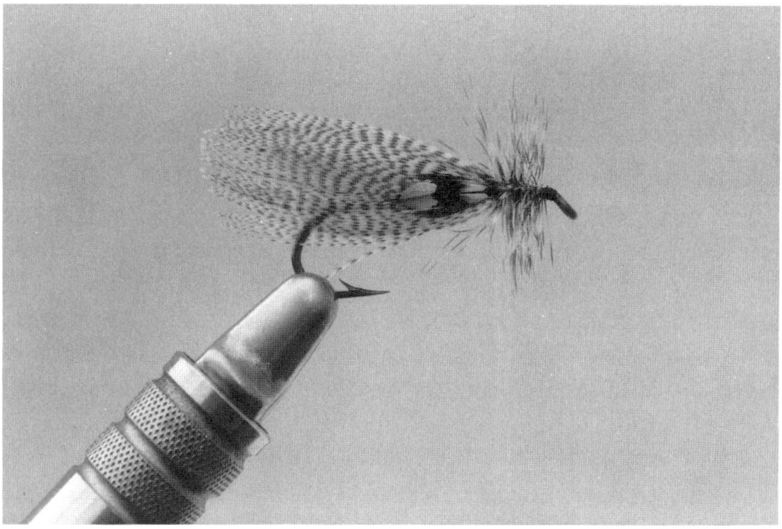

Tying the Hornberg

HOOK:	2x long nymph or dry fly, e.g., Mustad #9671, sizes 6-16
THREAD:	Black
BODY:	Flat silver tinsel
UNDERWING:	Yellow calf tail
OVERWING:	Mallard flank feathers
CHEEKS:	Jungle cock (or substitute)
HACKLE:	Grizzly

1. Attach the tinsel at the bend. Take the thread forward. Cover the shank of the hook with tinsel and tie off.
2. Attach a shank-length section of calf tail in the wing position.
3. Add mallard flank feathers to both sides of the hook so that the concave sides of the feathers face the shank.
4. Attach a jungle cock eye or substitute on each side. (Because the fly is something of a sentimental favorite to me, I use my dwindling supply of real jungle cock eyes on this pattern. Imitation eyes or other substitutes could, of course, be used. Some fly tiers omit the cheeks altogether.)
5. Attach a dry-fly quality grizzly hackle feather and wrap it, creating a full-hackled fly. Whip finish.

Blue-Winged Olive

If you don't live in Alaska (and maybe even if you do), I would be willing to bet that this is the last fly pattern you were expecting to read about in this book. Blue-Winged Olives, small dry flies, in Alaska? I love to despoil good myths, so I will be blunt: yes, there are mayflies in Alaska (but no, we don't live in igloos). According to my microscope and taxonomic keys the blue-winged olives up here are the same genus, Baetidae, as the ones in the Lower Forty-Eight. As far as the species go, well, I'll admit that I have no burning desire to delve into taxonomic keys at the species level, so I refer to all of them as blue-winged olives. The fish don't seem to mind.

Like their Lower Forty-Eight counterparts, they are most likely to appear on a gray, overcast day with its associated precipitation, ranging from a light drizzle to torrential downpour. (Even if you haven't fished in Alaska, you may realize that "gray, overcast" describes an awful lot of our summer days.) You may see blue-winged olives emerging anytime from June through September, but the best concentrations usually occur from the second week of July into the second week of September. In July they will typically begin coming off the water around five o'clock in the afternoon, but by September their start is usually closer to three.

I once spent six days on a medium-sized river near the Wood-Tikchik State Park area with two good friends and angling companions, Doug Kennemer and Dennis Rodgers, without enjoying a single day of sunshine, but the blue-winged olives arrived each day like clockwork. Invariably, the first rise or mayfly spotted would be within 10 minutes of three o'clock. It was so dependable that around two-thirty, we would snip off whatever nymph or subsurface pattern we were using and get rigged up with appropriate leaders and dry flies before the action began. Then we would experience continuous action, catching grayling and char for about three hours, often staying in much the same spot and standing within earshot of each other.

When fish are rising during an emergence of these mayflies, the technique to present them is straightforward—regardless of your approach, use a dead drift. With no rises or very few rises apparent, you'll likely do better if you impart some action to the fly,

Grayling taken on dry fly.

like the previously described twitch. As with many species of fish elsewhere, the smaller grayling, char, and trout tend to move about a pool or reach of stream and pick off the floating duns at random, while the larger fish set up established feeding spots and may rise at fairly regular intervals.

The size of the naturals that I have seen in Alaska range, in corresponding hook sizes, from about 14 to 18. Generally, but not always, hatching insects get smaller as the season progresses. (Less prevalent, but sometimes quite abundant in certain locales, are much larger mayflies that appear anytime from June through August. These are much more like the western green drake of the West, and when they are present the fish will readily take a Gray Wulff in sizes 8-10.) I realize that there are several dressings for Blue-Winged Olives, some with hackle-tip wings, flank-feather wings, or duck-quill wings. The dressing below is the one that I have used most consistently throughout the past six seasons.

Tying the Blue-Winged Olive

HOOK:	Dry fly, e.g., Mustad #94840, sizes 14-18
THREAD:	Olive
TAIL:	Medium dun hackle fibers
BODY:	Medium olive dubbing
WING:	Gray mallard quill
HACKLE:	Medium dun

1. On this type of fly I prefer to set the wings first and then tie the rest of the fly. So, from a matched pair of quills select two sections that are approximately the same width as the gap of the hook. Tie them in so that they are approximately the same height as the shank is long.
2. Wrap the thread back to the tail position and attach a tail of hackle fibers equal in length to that of the shank.
3. Cover the body, between the base of the tail and the base of the wings, with fine, tightly twisted dubbing.
4. Attach the hackle and make two wraps behind the wings and finish with as many wraps as possible in front of the wings. Whip finish.

Bomber

The Bomber is a popular Atlantic salmon dry-fly pattern, and it only seemed logical that it should do well in Alaska on steelhead, silver salmon, and rainbow trout. It hasn't yet produced a steelhead for me, but it has accounted for a number of silver salmon and many, many more rainbow trout, some of huge dimensions. I'm not sure if it was designed to be used as a waking pattern but that's how I use it here in Alaska.

Initially I used the original Bomber dressing which is made of natural deer hair, brown saddle hackle, and woodchuck hair wings, and it worked reasonably well for several seasons. A couple of seasons ago, however, I got a wild idea to tie some Bombers of a relatively small size in bright orange and lime green. The idea hit me as I watched an accomplished nymph fisherman take rainbow after rainbow from some rather tricky pocket water. I was amazed, not at the number of fish that he was catching, but at the number of rainbow trout that were coming up and hitting his bright orange strike indicator.

Later he changed to a bright green strike indicator, and the results were equally amazing. For every trout that he took, at least one, maybe two, rainbow trout would rise and hit the strike indicator. As soon as I returned home, I settled in at my tying table and tied a bunch of orange and green Bombers. The natural-colored ones I had previously been using were all on size 2 and 4 hooks, but these I tied on 6's, 8's, and even 10's.

Since that time I have caught lots of trout on these bright little Bombers, and they are now a staple of my dry fly box. They will take fish as they float dead drift, but they are most effective when they are cast so that they swing into the current and create a wake. Because of the strike indicator incident, I had thought that they would be most effective when fished dead drift, but that hasn't proven to be the case. As I think back to the time those fish were hitting the strike indicator, I believe that most of the hits occurred once his nymph and strike indicator began to drag or when the nymph hung up on the bottom causing the indicator to stall in mid-swing.

Throughout the season I still use the larger, size 2 to 4 Bombers for covering big water, but whenever I encounter pocket water that I think will hold a few trout I break out the smaller sizes, 6 to 10. I do try a few additional colors each season, and at this point I have ruled out yellow as a producer. A black Bomber with white hackle has crept fairly close to the first string lineup after only one season of use.

Tying the Green Bomber

HOOK:	1x long, 2x fine salmon dry fly, e.g., Mustad #90240, sizes 6-10
THREAD:	Bright green
TAIL:	White calf tail
BODY:	Bright lime green deer hair spun and trimmed
HACKLE:	Grizzly saddle hackle dyed olive, palmered
WING:	White calf tail

1. Attach a tail of calf tail and two saddle hackles. (Only one will be needed to palmer over the deer hair body, but if you cut it off while trimming the body or it breaks when you begin to wrap it, you'll be glad there's an extra hackle. If you don't need it, you can cut it off.)
2. Spin deer hair along the shank of the hook from the tail to a

point just behind the eye of the hook. Trim it so that it increases in taper from front to back.

3. Attach wings of calf tail so that they tilt slightly forward.
4. Palmer the saddle hackle over the length of the deer hair body. Tie off and whip finish.

NOTE: For the Orange Bomber I retain the white wing and tail and use bright orange deer hair for the body, orange thread, and grizzly hackle.

Little Yellow Stonefly

Little yellow stoneflies and, less commonly, aphid-green and olive ones can be seen along swift, rocky streams almost anywhere in Alaska during the months of June through mid-September. On streams where they are present, it's not uncommon to see some everyday during the summer, but they are rarely seen flying in dense concentrations. The exception to this rule occurs when you disturb some streamside vegetation where a mass of them have settled in to take cover. I remember cutting across a small island that sat right in the middle of long riffle. As I waded through the waist deep grass, thousands of these little stoneflies took to the air. There were so many that it seemed as though every blade of grass must have had one sitting on it. I have also witnessed similar occurrences when crashing through streamside alder bushes. Although you still may see a few flying around, cold, gray, drizzly days usually cause them to take refuge in the surrounding greenery where you have to shake them out to see if they're present.

Sunny days are different. It seems as though the female stoneflies pick the brightest, hottest days of midsummer to flit around near the surface of the water carrying their eggs. If hot and bright don't seem like appropriate words to describe Alaska, you have to recognize that it is not always cloudy and rainy in Alaska. Remember too, that by mid-June and on into July we experience nearly 24-hour daylight over most of the state. Furthermore, take into consideration that your average Alaskan flyfishers are wearing neoprene up to their armpits, topped off with a wool shirt. Now throw a windless, sunny day where it seems like noontime is five hours long into this equation, and you've got hot.

These are exactly the days when the little stoneflies spend too much time too close to the water, and grayling, char, and trout take advantage of them. And these are exactly the days when you want to be wading in the cold water with the tops of your waders rolled down, wearing only a t-shirt (with, of course, lots of insect repellent on the bare skin), and casting a Little Yellow Stonefly to rising fish.

The fishing is not difficult, and the fish do not get ultra-selective. This is probably why the Little Yellow Stonefly is often overlooked. You could use almost any small dry fly, such as an Elk Hair Caddis, and still catch fish, but if you use a Little Yellow Stone you'll catch more—most likely many more—fish.

The female stoneflies dance right over the surface of the water, sometimes only an inch or so away, and they will often drop right to the surface, skitter forward for a short distance and then take off again. Herein lies the answer as to why the fishing can be so easy—the fish don't have to be presented with a perfectly dead-drifting fly. In fact, many times it seems like they prefer to have the fly drag for a moment, leaving a small wake behind it, just as the naturals do when they perform their mini touch-and-go maneuver on the water's surface.

The Little Yellow Stonefly is in the same boat as the Blue-Winged Olive. You are probably well aware of the fly, especially if you fish in the western part of the country, but I doubt that you associate it at all with Alaska. I would be willing to bet that if you have some Little Yellow Stoneflies, they would be in one of the fly boxes you leave at home when you come to Alaska. Don't. You may not experience too many warm sunny days, but if you do, and the fish are rising regularly for these stones, you'll be very sorry if you don't have any.

Tying the Little Yellow Stonefly

HOOK:	2x long dry fly, e.g., Tiemco #2302, sizes 14-16
THREAD:	Yellow
TAG:	Fluorescent orange thread
BODY:	Bright yellow dubbing with palmered ginger hackle
WING:	Bright yellow elk hair
HACKLE:	Ginger

1. With several wraps of orange tying thread, make a tag on the hook's bend, slightly below the typical tie-in position for a tail.
2. Attach a ginger hackle at the tail position. Dub the body. Palmer the hackle forward and tie off.
3. Attach the wing just as you would for an Elk Hair Caddis. Tie in another ginger hackle and take three or four wraps over the band of thread that separates the closely trimmed head and the wing. Tie off and whip finish.

Rio Grande Trude

At various times during the fishing season, I need to take a break. Not necessarily from fishing, but from a type of fishing. It's easy to get into a rut and spend several successive outings doing nothing but straining with the rod as you attempt to cleanly lift the extra-fast sinking-tip line for the next cast, slightly ducking your head as the large-hooked fly zips by your ear, and then listening to the distinctive plop as something like a size 2, weighted Wooly Bugger hits the water. The fishing might be good, actually it could be very, very good, but I yearn for something different. And for me this usually means putting the eight-weight rod loaded with a sinking-tip back into its tube and rigging up a five-weight with a freshly-cleaned floating line, leader, and dry fly.

Making this change is refreshing both physically and for my psyche. The problem is that this need may not, and often does not, occur when fishing a dry fly is the most productive option. There may be nothing too much happening in the way of insect emergences, and the fish might not be too interested in big deer hair or waking patterns. When this happens, regardless of the time of day or season, I tie on a Rio Grande Trude. It's automatic. I don't even think about it. Why? Chalk it up to simple experience, a dead-drifted Trude has bailed me out on many occasions when all other surface patterns that I tried didn't work.

Specifically, I remember one outstanding afternoon on a reach of water I refer to as Ouzel Run. There's a rock outcropping right where I usually begin fishing this particular stretch of river and plastered on those rocks at about head height is a water ouzel's nest. I usually fish until I reach a second outcropping about 200 yards upstream, but this particular day I never made it. It was mid-June and I had spent the previous four days fishing for salmon and had decided that on this day I would fish dry flies with my five-weight, regardless of the outcome. I tried several different patterns without too much luck until I switched to a Trude. It was the hot ticket.

I'm not sure exactly how many rainbow trout I caught, but it seemed as though the only time I didn't get a strike was when I was tying on a fresh Trude to replace one that had been torn apart by the fish. This hot action, combined with a warm, windless day and an uncharacteristic absence of any biting insects that allowed me to fish in a t-shirt, caused me to lose all sense of time. I wasn't even close to the second outcropping of rocks, and my watch showed that six hours had passed. It was time to leave. This was by no means the only splendid day of fishing I have had while using a Trude, but it is without a doubt one of the most memorable afternoons of fishing that I have had anywhere anytime.

The only disadvantage I can see with the Trude pattern that I currently use is that a chenille body isn't the best for a dry fly. It doesn't take long before I am more concerned with keeping the fly floating than with getting a good drift. The pattern I use, by the way, is called the Rio Grande Trude because it's a Rio Grande tied in the Trude style. There are other Trudes, too, but the one that has most recently impressed me sports a lime green body. Its current popularity is largely attributed to Wyoming angler Reynolds Pomeroy, but its roots go farther east to the state of Michigan where, reports have it, it originated under the name of the Pass Lake Streamer. I have only used it on Alaskan waters for a season or two, and I'm not ready to endorse it as a valuable Alaska pattern, but the initial results look promising.

Tying the Rio Grande Trude

HOOK:	3x long streamer, e.g., Mustad #9672, sizes 8-14
THREAD:	Black
TAIL:	Golden pheasant tippet fibers
BODY:	Black chenille
WING:	White calf tail
HACKLE:	Brown

1. Attach a tail of golden pheasant tippet fibers. These should be approximately one and a half times the width of the hook gap.
2. Attach the chenille. Take the thread forward to a point three eye-widths behind the eye of the hook. Wrap the chenille forward and tie off.
3. Attach the calf tail wing, which should extend past the bend of the hook, even with the tips of the tail.
4. Attach the hackle and wrap forward. (If necessary to cover the remaining portion of the hook shank, use more than one hackle.) Tie off and whip finish.

Humpy

The Humpy wound up in this selection by edging out some other top-flight dry flies, most notably the Wulffs. In my mind I consider both the Humpies and the Wulffs to be types of flies rather than particular patterns, and the many variations of both are used quite frequently in Alaska. The Wulffs, though, have always had those certain intangible factors on their side which made them a classier fly to fish with than the Humpies. Sort of like the many unwarranted distinctions between white collar and blue collar workers that some people make automatically. Various Wulff patterns have enticed Atlantic salmon into striking, and in some circles Atlantic salmon are considered the preeminent game fish. Any fly regularly used for them then gets rated a notch above all others. Wulffs have also enticed some species of Pacific salmon into striking.

Humpies may have taken both Atlantic salmon and Pacific salmon, but they are not recognized as patterns for either. The Wulff patterns were created by the late Lee Wulff, who incidentally began his fishing in Alaska. In case you're very new to this sport or have been fishing on some planet other than earth, he was considered by some to be flyfishing's highest deity. In comparison, the Humpy's origins are a bit clouded, and depending upon who you talk to and what you read, was created by several different people, none of whom approach the status of Lee Wulff.

So why all this discussion of Wulffs when the fly up for consideration is a Humpy? Simple. I use both types of patterns, but when I took a long, thoughtful look back at all the dry-fly fishing—with particular attention paid to Wulffs and Humpies—I have done in Alaska, the conclusion was one-sided. I use more sizes and varieties of Humpies, fish them more often, catch more fish with them, and in most cases would select them for use over a Wulff. This may be a sort of back-handed way of showering a fly with praise, but if I had to choose between a Humpy and a Wulff to fish with in Alaska, I would choose the Humpy, and that in itself I consider to be very high praise.

For a long time I used Humpies only on fast, broken water when I needed an offering that would fulfill three criteria: be visible to the fish, be a good enough target to be seen racing through the dips and patches of white water, and be better than average in the floatability department. The Humpy fits the bill on all three counts. I still use the Humpy in that fast, broken water that many western fly anglers would consider good Humpy water, but I have come to learn, albeit kind of slowly, that Humpies will take fish in all kinds of water, including spooky rainbows or cutts in small, placid ponds.

I tie Humpies in a very wide range of sizes and a variety of colors. I have them as large as size 4, which I use to drift over the heads of shallow-holding silver salmon and salmon-sized rainbow trout. I use the mid-range sizes, 8–12, almost anywhere for any kind of fish that may come to the surface. The smaller ones, sizes 16 and 18, do a fine job on stillwaters and slower-moving sections of streams where the grayling are apt to get a little finicky about the size of a fly. Although I have tried them in lots of different colors, black is my favorite with red and bright yellow being real close runner-ups.

Feel free to experiment with the dressing below. I have tied Humpies with all different kinds of hollow hair—caribou, moose, elk, deer, antelope—and they have all performed well. Even after lots of repetition, I still don't like the way my Humpies turn out when compared with the creations tied by many other more talented fly tiers, but they seem to work just as well. So, if your Humpies don't look as good as those pretty pictures in the magazines and catalogs, don't worry, the fish up here in Alaska don't seem to mind at all.

Tying the Humpy

HOOK:	Dry fly, e.g., Mustad #94840, sizes 4-18
THREAD:	Black
TAIL:	Moose body hair, deer hair, or other very stiff hair
UNDERBODY:	Black floss or complete coverage with the tying thread
OVERBODY:	Same as tail
WING:	Natural deer hair or tips of the same hair as used for the overbody and tail
HACKLE:	Brown and grizzly

1. Cover the hook shank with thread and tie in a very thick clump of hair for the tail (thick and long enough to make the tail and a complete overbody). After measuring for the tail length, attach the butt ends of this hair at the midpoint of the hook shank and completely cover them with thread as you work back to the tail position. On very large sizes you may want to tie in some floss here to make the job of covering the hair easier.
2. Return the thread to the midpoint of the hook shank, covering the hair completely. Grasp two thirds of the material from the tail and fold it forward to the thread. Make several wraps over this material with the thread and secure it.
3. The tips of the hair will now be extending forward past the eye of the hook and can be lifted and separated with the thread using a figure-eight pattern to form wings. (If you are using a material other than deer hair for the tail and overbody, cut the ends and tie in a clump of deer hair for the wings. Lift and separate as above.)
4. Attach the two hackles. Make two or three wraps behind the wing and continue wrapping forward to the eye. Tie off and whip finish.

Chapter 5: Topwater Models
Fly and Season

	JAN	FEB	MAR	APR	MAY	JUN	JUL	AUG	SEP	OCT	NOV	DEC
Katmai Slider						XXX	XXX	XXX	XXX	XX		
Simple Shrew						XXX	XXX	XXX	XXX	X		
Hornberg					XX	XXX	XXX	XXX	X			
Blue-Winged Olive							XX	XXX	XX			
Bomber						XXX		X	XXX			
Little Yellow Stonefly						XX	XXX	XXX	XX			
Rio Grande Trude						XXX	XXX	XXX	X			
Humpy						XX	XXX	XXX	XXX			

Chapter 5: Topwater Models
Fly and Species

	KS	RS	CS	PS	SS	RT	ST	CT	CH	LT	AG	NP	SF
Katmai Slider					X	X	X		X		X		
Simple Shrew						X			X		X	X	
Hornberg						X		X		X	X		
Blue-Winged Olive						X		X	X		X		
Bomber					X	X		X			X		
Little Yellow Stonefly						X			X		X		
Rio Grande Trude						X		X		X	X		
Humpy						X		X	X	X	X		

KS = King Salmon, RS = Red or Sockeye Salmon, CS = Chum Salmon, PS = Pink Salmon, SS = Silver or Coho Salmon, RT = Rainbow Trout, ST = Steelhead, CT = Cutthroat Trout, CH = Arctic Char/Dolly Varden, LT = Lake Trout, AG = Arctic Grayling, NP - Northern Pike, SF = Sheefish

Lake Leech, Pin Head Muddler, Crowe Beetle, Mosquito Larva, Simple Midge, Partridge-and-Yellow

Chapter 6
Stillwater Specialties

If you come to Alaska and debit your bank account for the funds needed to stay at a deluxe wilderness lodge for that once-in-a-lifetime trip, you probably won't fish many lakes. When people imagine their dream trip to Alaska, they conjure up images of taking rainbow trout from picturesque streams studded with salmon and grizzly bears. The lodges and outfitters recognize this and do their best to make these dreams become realities. However, this does not mean that Alaska has a lack of lakes in which to cast a fly.

In fact, for every stream there are usually many lakes in the vicinity that could be fished although they may not contain the same species, particularly anadromous ones, that attract all the attention in moving water. Differences in species aside, most anglers just prefer not to fish stillwaters when there is running water nearby. I'll admit that I have a preference for the character of streams, but I enjoy variety and rarely pass up the chance to fish a lake.

Flyfishing Alaskan stillwater.

Besides, there are some people (me for one) who actually live up here year round, and in the southcentral part of the state where I live stream fishing isn't altogether that good—or legal—during mid- to late May when the lakes are beginning to open up. This part of the state is studded with easy-to-get-to lakes that act as early season relief valves for local flyfishers. At times the fishing can be good enough to make me wonder why I spend so much time in the nether regions of the state searching for fish when I can catch whoppers along the road system north and south of Anchorage. Which brings up another point. Some of us who live up here aren't wealthy and can't afford to jump into a floatplane any time we want to head out to those remote places where every fish is a potential magazine cover. And when the road-accessible salmon streams start attracting crowds, the roadside lakes offer salvation and solitude for us locals.

Whether you prefer to glide along in a canoe, wade the shallows, or paddle out in a float tube, you should at least take a look at Alaska's lakes. While the action on streams is often concentrated around the return of a particular anadromous species, lakes offer an extended season, which may begin as early as mid-May and possibly stretch into early November. In Alaska's lakes you can find rainbow, lake, and cutthroat trout, char, grayling, northern pike, and a landlocked variety of the sockeye salmon known as kokanee.

While the following patterns are what I consider to be lake-only flies, there are many other fly patterns scattered throughout the other chapters that are quite suitable for stillwater use.

Lake Leech

The Lake Leech meets all the requirements for consideration as a great Alaskan fly pattern. The only material needed to tie it, other than the thread, hook, and lead, is marabou, which is inexpensive and easily obtained. The tying procedure can be mastered by even the novice fly tier, and most importantly, it consistently catches fish throughout Alaska. Primarily a lake pattern, it will work in streams and rivers, but among my fly assortments it is allotted space only in the boxes that I reserve for fishing stillwaters. It is a preeminent pattern for many of Alaska's fish species that inhabit lakes, including rainbow trout, lake trout, char, and grayling. It is best fished with a slow strip or hand-twist retrieve. I have used many different colors over the years, but the only two I now carry are olive and purple. Like many flies tied and fished in Alaska, it is usually weighted, but here a strong case can be made for carrying unweighted as well as weighted patterns as illustrated by the following memorable outing.

It was the first of September and finding many of the local streams running high due to an onslaught of late August rains, Duane Marler and I decided to pump up our float tubes and try out one of our favorite lakes. The wind began to pick up, and it rained lightly as we hiked into the lake. Under those conditions, Duane made the prudent decision to outfit himself with a sinking line. My rod was rigged with a floating line, and rather than change I figured that I would throw a big mouse pattern along the shoreline weed growth in hopes of finding a big, hungry fish in the shallows. Success didn't seem likely, and predictably, the big floater drew no attention. Duane meanwhile had landed a fish or two, and I decided that if I was going to have any action at all I would have to switch to some type of subsurface imitation.

Rather than switching to a sinking-tip line, I stayed with the floating line, lengthened my leader to 12 feet and tied on a size 8, weighted Olive Lake Leech. One 10-inch rainbow managed to inhale the fly, but on most retrieves I was greeted with nothing other than the tug of aquatic vegetation. The weeds grew from the bottom to a distance of three or four feet below the water's surface, and retrieving the fly slowly did nothing more than allow the fly to sink into the tangle of weeds. I shortened the leader, but similar results prevailed. Then spying the different colored head of one of the leeches in my box—indicating that it was an unweighted pattern—I again lengthened my leader to about 12 feet and tied it on. The difference was dramatic and remarkable. I could now retrieve the fly very slowly without fouling in the weeds, and I began to catch rainbows—lots of them, enough so that now Duane was getting interested in what fly I was using.

In the intervening time the weather had gone from bad to worse to completely outrageous. Duane had to paddle close enough so that our tubes nearly touched to be heard above the noise made by the wind, rain, and waves lashing up and over our tubes. After his inquiry about the fly I was using, I handed over a weighted Olive Lake Leech. The only unweighted one that I had was still attached to my line and still catching fish. Fishing side-by-side, both using floating lines, the unweighted version continued to catch fish while the weighted one rarely drew a strike before it gathered a bunch of trailing vegetation.

The day became a memorable one not so much because of the disparity of our catch rates, but instead due to the just plain awful weather that we endured in our float tubes. Regardless of the weather, the day did illustrate once again that the Lake Leech is a dynamite pattern when fished in Alaska's lakes, and while 90% of the time the weighted version is most effective, it pays to have at least one unweighted Lake Leech in your box.

Tying the Olive Lake Leech

HOOK:	3x long streamer, Mustad #9672, sizes 6-10
WEIGHT:	.025″ lead
THREAD:	Black
TAIL:	Olive marabou
BODY:	Olive marabou twisted and wrapped

1. Wrap the hook shank with lead from a spot directly above the hook point to a distance of two eye-widths behind the eye. Secure, leaving the thread at the tail position.
2. Attach the tip of a marabou feather so that it extends as a tail approximately the same length as the shank of the hook. Take the thread forward to the eye of the hook.
3. Holding the remaining section of the marabou feather by the butt section of the stem, twist it several times and then wrap it forward, as you would a piece of chenille, to the thread. Tie off and whip finish.

Pin Head Muddler

On one of my first lake fishing trips in Alaska, the person with me was catching way too many fish. Roughly translated, this means he was catching fish, and I wasn't. Admitting that I had little knowledge of the local traditions and tactics, I yelled to him, from a fair distance, "What fly are you using?" His head was turning back and forth as he made a cast so I could only understand the middle part of his reply, the rest being drowned out as his head turned away from me to watch his back cast. Actually, I only understood, or thought I understood, two words—pin head.

Until that time in my life I had not been called a pin head nor heard of a fly called the pin head. I did know of a fly called a Picket Pin, and as a matter of fact, I had some in my vest. I asked again. The reply was again muffled by the distance and the wind, but this time it was much shorter. Whether it was because the words cut through the wind better than whatever else he said or because I was listening for the term, I'm not sure, but this time I definitely heard him say pin head. At this point I figured he was either calling me a pin head, telling me his fly was the size of a pin head, or telling me that the name of the fly was pin head.

This guy didn't seem to be in the mood for any further discussion, so I followed what I thought was the most logical process. I spent the rest of the evening alternating between a Picket Pin and a size 22 Trico spinner. I figured if this "pin head" was a fly pattern it might be a version of the Picket Pin, and the Picket Pin might also prove to be as successful as whatever it was he was using. I tried the tiny Trico because it was the closest thing that I had to the size of a pin head. After a while I even clipped the wings off of it to make it appear even smaller. The Picket Pin accounted for a few small fish, and nothing even made a pass at the Trico, with or without its wings.

That evening as we drove back into town—without alluding to the notion that I thought he might have called me a pin head—I found out that the fly he had been using was a Pin Head Muddler. The fly was nothing more than a very small, sparse Muddler Minnow.

Its small size and trim appearance have a lot to do with its effectiveness. On many occasions I have tried a standard Muddler

Minnow pattern, tied much larger and dressed fuller, and it has never even come close to working as well as the Pin Head Muddler does in lakes. After years of using it with great success, I still have no idea what the fish think it is. Maybe it represents a drowned damselfly or a small injured fish or just something that looks good to eat.

I usually have best results with it during the afternoon on a calm, sunny day when nothing seems to be happening. I don't use any fly floatant so after a little bit of use it rides in the water rather than right on top, but the deer hair keeps it from sinking more than an inch or two. I almost always fish it the same way, two short twitches and then a pause until the disturbance it has caused disappears. Rolling strikes usually occur just as you begin to twitch it after a pause. Rainbow trout, grayling, and whitefish are susceptible to this fly, and a couple of seasons ago I had two memorable June days of fishing for lake trout at a lake off of the Denali Highway where I used nothing but the Pin Head Muddler. None of the lakers weighed more than a couple of pounds, but there were rarely times throughout the day when I wasn't fighting a fish.

Tying the Pin Head Muddler

HOOK:	2x long streamer, e.g., Tiemco #5262, size 12
THREAD:	Black
TAIL:	Mottled turkey fibers
BODY:	Gold mylar tinsel
WING:	Mottled turkey
HEAD:	Fine textured deer hair spun and trimmed close with only a sparse collar

1. Attach a tail equal in length to that of the hook gap and tie in the tinsel.
2. Take the thread forward, leaving enough room behind the eye of the hook to spin a deer hair head. Wrap the tinsel forward and tie off. At this same point, attach the wing of turkey quill.
3. Spin deer hair on the remaining bare portion of the hook. Trim the head so that it is very small and rounded with only a few hairs left uncut sweeping back with the wing. Whip finish.

Crowe Beetle

Yes, I know, this is a dry fly. So why isn't it in that chapter? Well for starters, my Crowe Beetles do not necessarily always float—especially after I've caught a few fish with them. Sometimes they even seem to be more enticing to the fish when they become waterlogged and sink at such a slow rate that they seem to be suspended—not sinking—an inch or two below the surface. Also, due to their record of accomplishments, they are one of the last flies that I would choose when fishing an Alaskan stream. But—and this is an important but—I wouldn't fish an Alaskan lake without having some of them with me.

According to my old college text, *An Introduction to the Study of Insects*, beetles are by far the largest order of insects, and as many as 30,000 species occur in the United States. With numbers like this it would seem reasonable that you could tie on a beetle almost anytime anywhere and have a good chance of imitating something that may find its way into the water and into a fish's mouth. This indeed seems to be the case on Alaska's stillwaters. Even though there are thousands of beetles that don't necessarily look like a Crowe Beetle, there's a heck of a lot of them that could be described as small, dark, and sort of round. That's exactly how I would describe the Crowe Beetle.

I used to pull out a Crowe Beetle only when I was fishing close to lily pads. I often found small, dark beetles crawling around on the lily pads, and the fish were almost always receptive to a beetle imitation. Now I am less selective about where I use the bogus beetle, and the fish have responded positively by taking it even when I'm not fishing near lily pads. About the only place that I haven't used the beetle with any success has been out in open water far from shore. Near any type of weed growth, overhanging branches, or thick shore-side bushes, if any pattern will interest a fish, a Crowe Beetle will. Originally, I had only used it during the warmest part of the summer from early July into the beginning of August, but I have since used it with an equal degree of success as early as mid-May right after ice-out and as late as the end of September.

My favorite technique with the Crowe Beetle is to cast it into a nook or cranny created by vegetation or get it as far back as possible underneath overhanging branches. Then I inch it forward so slowly that the movement is barely perceptible. If after a while the beetle sinks, I use this to my advantage rather than tying on a fresh imitation. I'll cast into the same likely looking spots and just let it sink without any retrieve at all. The strikes will often be nothing more than a slight visible twitch in the floating part of the leader.

The Crowe Beetle is mainly a rainbow trout and grayling fly, but there are times when lake trout and other char also take it. The latter are most notably attracted to it when they are feeding on floating snails. I have encountered lake trout and char feeding on floating snails many times, and the Crowe Beetle seems to be a close enough representation that I haven't had to carry a snail pattern. When it is taken as a beetle, it's general enough to imitate any of them that might fall into the water. Even with no naturals around, it seems to attract fish in the same universal way a Black Ant attracts stream-dwelling fish. As to why it works so well in lakes but not streams, I don't have an explanation, but I do know that I will not go lake fishing without it.

Tying the Crowe Beetle

HOOK:	Dry fly, e.g., Mustad #94840, size 16
THREAD:	Black
BODY:	Black dubbing
OVERBODY:	Black deer hair
HEAD:	Black deer trimmed
LEGS:	Three deer hair fibers on each side left untrimmed

1. Attach a clump of deer hair, butt ends forward, just behind the eye of the hook. Covering the deer hair, work the thread back to the tail position. There should be at least two shank-lengths of deer hair extending beyond the bend of the hook.
2. Cover the body, from the tail position to just behind the eye of the hook, with black dubbing.
3. Grasp the hair extending beyond the hook bend, bring it forward, and tie off just behind the eye. Trim the deer hair as you would the head of an Elk Hair Caddis but leave three hairs on each side. These should be left longer and positioned at right angles to the hook shank to represent legs. Tie off and whip finish.

Mosquito Larva

The effectiveness of the Mosquito Larva is largely due to the fact that, as an impressionistic pattern, it transcends its name. While you are undoubtedly familiar with the adult, blood-sucking variety of mosquito, the Mosquito Larva fly pattern does not imitate just the subadult form of that insect. It can be taken for a number of insects that, at one time or another, may be found near the surface of stillwaters.

It may represent the larva of a phantom midge from the family Chaoboridae—an entity not too well known among flyfishers. Without stretching the imagination too much, it might also mimic an emerging Chironomidae pupa. Dip a gallon of water from the surface of a lake in Alaska, or anywhere for that matter, and you are liable to see lots of organisms that a fish might mistake a Mosquito Larva for. Regardless of its name or what it represents, the Mosquito Larva consistently fools fish.

It works best for me during the month of June. Its performance from ice-out until the end of May is spotty, and by early July its seems like the fish are on the prowl for a more substantial meal. During June, though, it's one of the first flies out of my box.

Patience is the only prerequisite to catching fish with the Mosquito Larva. If you are in a hurry or like to do things fast, put on a streamer or something else to keep yourself occupied, because the key word with this fly is slow. Dead drifting it is the most effective strategy. The best days are ones that have enough breeze to slightly ripple the water's surface. On these days I'll use a floating line with a 10-foot leader, cast perpendicular to the wind, and just let the ripples slowly drag the line and the fly through the water. Occasionally I'll pull sharply on the line to cause the fly to twitch and also to take some of the slack out of the belly of the line. "Occasionally", here, means once every 30 seconds or, even better, once every minute. If you don't think this is a long time, time it with the sweep second hand of your watch. You won't believe how long a minute can last while you're staring at a belly forming in your line and looking for the slightest indication that something has taken your Mosquito Larva.

Grayling and rainbow trout are both regularly caught with this fly, while char don't seem to be particularly fond of it. Of all the species, lake-bound cutthroat trout seem to be the most susceptible to the Mosquito Larva in combination with the slow fishing technique. In fact, the majority of the biggest cutts that I have caught in Alaska's stillwaters were fooled with a slowly fished Mosquito Larva.

Tying the Mosquito Larva

HOOK:	Dry fly, e.g., Mustad #94840, sizes 14-18
THREAD:	White
BODY:	Stripped peacock herl
THORAX:	Peacock herl
ANTENNAE:	Grizzly hackle fibers

1. At the bend of the hook, attach a peacock herl that has been stripped of its fibers. Take the thread forward to a point about two eye-widths behind the eye of the hook. Wrap the herl forward to form a body and tie off.
2. Attach a piece of unstripped peacock herl. Also attach a sparse clump of grizzly hackle fibers so that they extend forward beyond the eye of the hook.
3. Wrap the peacock herl forward, creating a thorax. Tie off and whip finish.

Simple Midge

"There we were. Fish were rising all around us, and we tried every single dry fly that we had but couldn't get them to bite. They were eating these tiny, little itty-bitty things that were all over the top of the water."

You would be amazed how many times I've heard this story in my flyfishing and fly tying classes or in general conversation with other flyfishers. They often say it with a sense of astonishment that somehow implies these fish should know better. After all, these are big Alaskan fish and they're supposed to swim around in the murky depths attacking large colorful lures. They are not supposed to hang out just below the surface daintily sipping in objects that cause people with normal vision to reach for a magnifying glass. Evidently, a lot of the fish in Alaska haven't read the appropriate literature and fail to realize that their temperament should be bolder and their tastes more cannibalistic.

When these mass midge emergences take place, any fish—even lake trout—may become selective and only take flies that approximate the size of the naturals. Lake-bound grayling are notorious for this, which makes it even more frustrating for some anglers because grayling are supposed to be easy to catch. However frustrating it may be, the solution is quite simple. Give them the little, itty-bitty flies that they want.

The fly that I give them a look at I refer to as the Simple Midge. As its name suggests, there's not much to it, just a dubbed fur body with two or three turns of hackle. Although I have, with appropriate magnification, observed many different colored midges I haven't found it necessary to duplicate the colors. I stick with gray muskrat underbody fur, and it seems to work fine regardless of the color of the natural. It has been my experience that while fishing Alaska's lakes during times of midge abundance, matching the size of the natural is far more important than duplicating the color.

Fish will often cruise just below the surface rising at regular enough intervals to give you a good idea of the specific track they are headed along. Once this has been determined, cast the fly so that the fish's path will intercept the fly. This sounds real chancy, but in practice it is really not that difficult to do. You will not be able to see the fly so you'll have to react to any rise or bulge in the

Stillwater midge fishing.

surface near the end of your leader. If the fish happens to rise well short of your fly, by three feet or so, give the fly a twitch, and you'll often experience another quick rise as the fish turns and takes the fly.

There are almost always at least a few midges emerging from Alaska's lakes any time the water is ice-free. Sporadic emergence intervals and low densities will rarely cause the fish to become selective, and there are times when midges literally cover the surface of the water and the fish continue to take a variety of patterns. Selectivity to midges primarily occurs during the months of July and August in the southcentral region of Alaska, but I have occasionally witnessed it as early as mid-May on lakes in the Matanuska-Susitna Valley. If it happens while you're out there, it will be awfully frustrating if you don't have a couple of these little, itty-bitty midges.

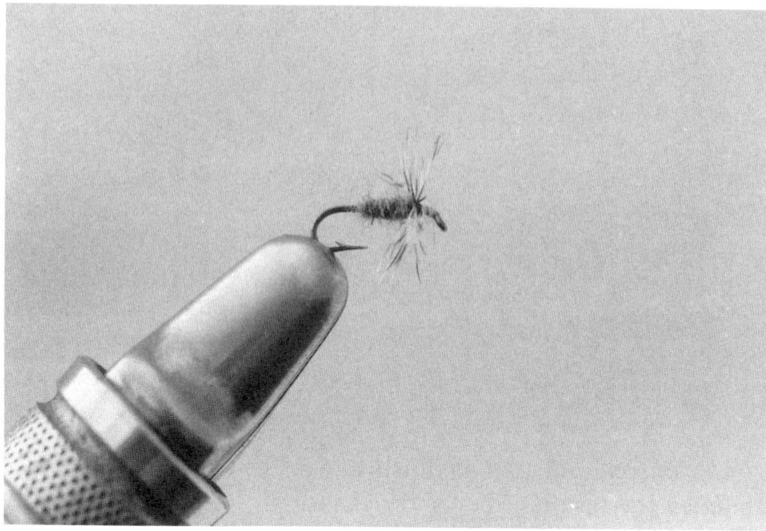

Tying the Simple Midge

HOOK:	Dry fly or midge, e.g., Mustad #94840 or Tiemco #500U, sizes 18-22
THREAD:	White
BODY:	Dubbed gray muskrat fur, tapered so that there is more bulk in the thoracic region
HACKLE:	Grizzly

1. Dub a body of fine muskrat underbody fur.
2. Attach a grizzly hackle and make two or three wraps with it. Tie off and whip finish.

Partridge-and-Yellow

Why the Partridge-and-Yellow wet fly? First of all, I happen to like soft hackle patterns very much, and secondly, this one has produced fish from lakes for as long as I have been fishing in Alaska, often when other patterns work marginally, if at all.

Why yellow? Well, I used an array of colors—claret, olive, red, orange, white, insect green, and yellow—for a long time. Although I wasn't keeping an actual head count, yellow always seemed to work better than the other colors, so at one point I decided to keep track. In a rather crude study, I logged the amount of time (over a span of two seasons) I fished the various colors of soft hackle flies. I fished with them under all weather conditions during the season from start to finish, and at the end of two seasons I tabulated the results. They showed that the yellow dressing outdistanced white, its closest competitor, by a margin of four to one. I realize that from an experimental design standpoint there are all kinds of intangibles and flaws inherent in this type of comparison, but I was fishing rather than writing a thesis, so the results are good enough for me.

There could be a logical explanation for why the yellow produces more fish than other colors. The soft hackle is one of those general impressionistic patterns that could be perceived as many different living organisms that a fish might choose to eat. Furthermore, two of the more abundant aquatic stillwater insects in Alaska are the backswimmers (Notonectidae) and waterboatmen (Corixidae), and coincidentally these insects just happen to often have a yellowish-creamy-brown overall color which might be imitated by a yellow-bodied, brown-hackled fly such as the Partridge-and-Yellow.

I have seen small rainbow trout chase and consume waterboatmen and backswimmers, and I have found these insects in the mouths of larger fish I've caught. However, I've never been pleased with the results of some of the more bulky and realistic patterns that imitate these insects. Maybe the Partridge-and-Yellow does a better job of mimicking them than the realistic patterns or maybe the fish just happen to like this pattern. I'm not sure, but I do keep a supply of Partridge-and-Yellows in a fly box which remains permanently in a pocket of my float tube, and I

catch rainbow trout with them consistently.

Typically I fish this pattern with a floating line and a leader of nine feet or longer. I give the fly plenty of time to sink and then I retrieve it in sharp, evenly spaced strips of about six inches. On occasions when this doesn't work and I want to fish the fly deeper, I'll switch to a sinking-tip line with a leader of about four feet and repeat the same procedure. On any day, even if the fishing happens to be very slow, a Partridge-and-Yellow will almost always turn at least a fish or two for me. Usually it does much better than that.

While Partridge-and-Yellow is its official name, it's commonly called a yellow soft hackle. As far as the partridge part goes, I have tied some with real partridge feathers, but the majority of the time I substitute spruce grouse or ptarmigan, both locally abundant in Alaska. The birds may be different, but once the hackle has been put on the fly the difference is difficult to detect. The fish don't seem to mind at all. I think the important point is to find the appropriate brown mottled color and then use the soft, webby, feathers regardless of what kind of bird they come from.

Tying the Partridge-and-Yellow

HOOK:	2x strong wet fly, e.g., Tiemco #3769, sizes 10-16
THREAD:	Yellow
BODY:	Yellow floss rear two-thirds, front third fine, pale yellow dubbing
HACKLE:	Partridge (or spruce grouse or ptarmigan)

1. Attach the yellow floss at the bend of the hook. Cover the rear two-thirds of the hook shank with floss and tie off.
2. Attach a partridge body feather by the butt of the stem so that it extends forward beyond the eye of the hook.
3. Over this stem, add dubbing to the front third of the hook shank.
4. In front of the dubbing and directly behind the eye of the hook, take two turns of the partridge hackle. Tie off and whip finish.

Chapter 6: Stillwater Specialties
Fly and Season

	JAN	FEB	MAR	APR	MAY	JUN	JUL	AUG	SEP	OCT	NOV	DEC
Lake Leech, olive							XX	XXX	XXX	XXX		
Lake Leech, purple					XX	XXX	XXX					
Pin Head Muddler						X	XXX	XXX	X			
Crowe Beetle					XX	XXX	XXX	XXX	XXX			
Mosquito Larva					X	XXX	X					
Simple Midge							XXX	XXX				
Partridge-and-Yellow					XX	XXX	XXX	XXX	XXX	X		

Chapter 6: Stillwater Specialties
Fly and Species

	KS	RS	CS	PS	SS	RT	ST	CT	CH	LT	AG	NP	SF
Lake Leech, olive						X		X	X	X	X		
Lake Leech, purple						X		X	X	X	X		
Pin Head Muddler						X				X	X		
Crowe Beetle						X		X	X	X	X		
Mosquito Larva						X		X		X	X		
Simple Midge						X		X		X	X		
Partridge-and-Yellow						X		X	X	X	X		

KS = King Salmon, RS = Red or Sockeye Salmon, CS = Chum Salmon, PS = Pink Salmon, SS = Silver or Coho Salmon, RT = Rainbow Trout, ST = Steelhead, CT = Cutthroat Trout, CH = Arctic Char/Dolly Varden, LT = Lake Trout, AG = Arctic Grayling, NP - Northern Pike, SF = Sheefish

Appendix A
Flies For Saltwater

Back in 1988 when I was writing the chapter on saltwater flyfishing for *Flyfishing Alaska*, I was in the rather unusual situation of being where not of a lot of other flyfishers had tread. I had flyfished extensively in Prince William Sound, less so in other parts of Alaska's saltwater, and in all those travels I had not once caught another saltwater flyrodder in the act. The only other flyfishers I witnessed flinging a fly into the salt were those I happened to be fishing with, and for many of them these outings were their first. I thought that with time things would change and I would see more saltwater flyfishers.

Things haven't changed that much, and I still haven't encountered another flyfisher fishing in saltwater. From reports I receive, I know there are some devout saltwater flyfishers who regularly fish the waters around Kodiak Island. Farther down in southeast Alaska, there are anglers who have been flyfishing the salt for years. I have had only limited contact with individuals from either of these groups and claim even less familiarity with their home-grown fly patterns.

During my saltwater excursions I rely heavily upon the same patterns that I use for salmon fishing in freshwater, and I had hoped to learn some new patterns and share them here. Of the few flies that have trickled back to me, many are well thought out and well-tied creations, but in the limited amount of time I have soaked them in the salt, the results weren't anything outstanding. In fact some of the most beautiful creations performed decidedly worse than my freshwater salmon patterns.

I am now inclined to believe that finding the fish and getting a fly in front of them is far more important than the specific fly pattern. As you will see, the only adjustment that I might make on my freshwater flies is to tie them on corrosion-resistant hooks such as the Mustad #3407 or #34007, the Tiemco 800S, and others from manufacturers such as Daiichi, Gamakatsu, and Kamasan. I've only experimented with these last three brands for the past season or two and don't feel that I've had enough water time with them yet to make specific recommendations.

Perhaps in the future I'll find more flyfishers in the salt and discover some patterns designed just for the Alaskan saltwater that are consistent producers. In the meantime, here's an annotated list of previously described patterns that work well for me.

Alevin

The Alevin sees limited saltwater use. There are times, however, when either sea-run cutthroat trout or Dolly Varden gather at the mouths of pink salmon spawning streams to feed on outgoing fry, and it is deadly at these times.

Blue Smolt

The Blue Smolt can be used with good success on cutts and dollies wherever freshwaters dump smolt into the ocean. It's also effective when quickly stripped through estuaries once adult silver salmon have returned.

White Wooly Bugger

With no idea what they take it for, the White Wooly Bugger has always been a good producer of rockfish when I can find them in shallow enough water to reach with a fly. I substitute a Mustad #34007 hook for the Mustad #9672 hook described in the freshwater dressing. The fly comes out looking a little chunkier but it works.

Flash Fly

A great all-around saltwater pattern for cutts, dollies, silvers, and king salmon.

Hot Pink Sparkle Shrimp

An excellent pattern for silver salmon when they can be found in shallow intertidal areas. When I am tying Sparkle Shrimp to be used in the salt, I use a Mustad #3407 rather than a Mustad #36890.

Chartreuse Everglow Fly

The Chartreuse Everglow Fly ranks right up there with the Flash Fly as a great all-around saltwater pattern. It's most effective on silver and king salmon.

Gold Comet

I tie the saltwater Gold Comet just as sparsely as I do the one for sockeye salmon and have found it to be dynamite on cutthroats in estuaries. I tie a supply of Gold Comets on Mustad #3407 hooks for saltwater use.

Lefty's Deceiver

Although it is more commonly associated with saltwater fly-fishing in warmer climates, Deceivers will work along Alaska's coastline for any species of fish that preys on smaller fish.

Appendix B
Keys To The Tables

Fly and Season Tables

In the Fly and Season tables you will notice that the months are broken down into three time periods, designated by three X's. Because of things like weather, water conditions, and the variability of run timing, dividing a month into its more logical four separate weeks can be like splitting hairs. It is more realistic to break the month into three ten-day periods that coincide with the familiar monthly prefixes of early, mid, and late. A column with all three X's represents the entire month, an X at the left of the column represents the first ten days of the month, an X at the right the last ten days, and two X's encompass a twenty-day period of either the first through the 20th day of the month or the 11th through the 30th day of the month, depending upon where the X's begin and end.

Fly and Species Tables

In the Fly and Species tables, the two-letter designations represent the following:

KS	king salmon (*Oncorhynchus tshawytscha*)
RS	sockeye or red salmon (*Oncorhynchus nerka*)
CS	chum salmon (*Oncorhynchus keta*)
PS	pink salmon (*Oncorhynchus gobuscha*)
SS	silver or coho salmon (*Oncorhynchus kisutch*)
RT	rainbow trout (*Oncorhynchus mykiss*)
ST	steelhead (*Oncorhynchus mykiss*)
CT	cutthroat trout (*Oncorhynchus clarki*)
CH	Arctic char/Dolly Varden (*Salvelinus alpinus/Salvelinus malma*)
LT	lake trout (*Salvelinus namaycush*)
AG	Arctic grayling (*Thymallus arcticus*)
NP	northern pike (*Esox lucius*)
SF	sheefish (*Stenodus leucichthys*)

References

In any work dealing with fly patterns, a certain amount of research into the literature has to be done to be certain of names, origins, and original dressings, and also to verify the habits, ranges, and behavior of the organisms that they may imitate. Although not all of the following were actually cited in the text of this book, they were used in some form or another to gather or verify information presented here.

Alaska Flyfishers. *Fly Patterns of Alaska.* Portland, Oregon: Frank Amato Publications, 1983.

Bates, Joseph D. Jr. *Streamers And Bucktails The Big Fish Flies.* New York: Knopf, 1979.

Borror, Donald J., Dwight M. DeLong, and Charles A. Triplehorn. *An Introduction to the Study of Insects.* New York: Holt, Rinehart and Winston, 1976, fourth edition.

Brooks, Charles E. *The Trout And The Stream.* New York: Crown, 1974.

Dennis, Jack. *Western Trout Fly Tying Manual.* Jackson Hole, Wyoming: Snake River Books, 1974.

Ferguson, Bruce, Les Johnson, and Pat Trotter. *Fly Fishing for Pacific Salmon.* Portland, Oregon: Frank Amato Publications, 1985.

Fulsher, Keith. *Tying and Fishing the Thunder Creek Series.* New York: Freshet Press, 1973.

Kaufmann, Randall. *The Fly Tyer's Nymph Manual.* Portland, Oregon: Western Fisherman's Press, 1986.

Leiser, Eric. *The Book of Fly Patterns.* New York: Knopf, 1987.

Merritt, Richard W. and Kenneth W. Cummins, eds. *An Introduction to the Aquatic Insects of North America.* Dubuque, Iowa: Kendall/Hunt, 1989, second edition.

Morrow, James E. *The Freshwater Fishes of Alaska.* Anchorage, Alaska: Alaska Northwest Publishing Co., 1980.

Pennak, Robert W. *Fresh-Water Invertebrates of the United States.* New York: John Wiley & Sons, 1989, third edition.

Route, Anthony J. *Flyfishing Alaska.* Boulder, Colorado: Johnson Books, 1989.

Taylor, Tamra. *Species List of Alaskan Birds, Mammals, Freshwater and Anadromous Fish, Amphibians, Reptiles, and Commercially Important Invertebrates.* U.S. Department of Agriculture, Forest Service, Alaska Region, Report #82, 1979.

Wiggins, G. B. *Larvae of the North American Caddisfly Genera.* Toronto: University of Toronto Press, 1977.

Index